T0171642

What Love Can Do

Recollected Stories of Slavery and
Freedom in New Orleans and the
Surrounding Area

By
Arthur Mitchell

Collected and Edited by Gayle Nolan

BALBOA.
PRESS

A DIVISION OF HAY HOUSE

ISBN: 978-1-4525-4624-7 (sc)
ISBN: 978-1-4525-4623-0 (e)

Library of Congress Control Number: 2012901050

Balboa Press books may be ordered through booksellers or by contacting:

Balboa Press
A Division of Hay House
1663 Liberty Drive
Bloomington, IN 47403
www.balboapress.com
1-(877) 407-4847

Printed in the United States of America

Balboa Press rev. date: 2/20/2012

Table of Contents

Introduction

This volume of stories written by Arthur Mitchell came to me through one of the students I taught in a freshman composition course at Delgado Community College in New Orleans. A non-traditional student, Teryl Mitchell had decided to enter college in her mid-thirties, after being out of high school for some years. Having had little or no preparation for college, Teryl struggled with grammar, spelling, and punctuation, and as a result, had failed in her first attempt at English 101. Discouraged, she confided in my supervisor that she would have to drop out of college because she would never pass English. Instead, my supervisor suggested that Teryl enroll in my special section of English 101, where she would receive more direct attention.

With her first essay, I immediately recognized a natural writer in Teryl---someone who could make a story come alive, who could make the reader care about what she was saying. The mechanics were poor, but I told Teryl in our first conference that was something we could work on. I was more excited about her ability to write. Teryl told me that she had inherited her natural talent from her father, who wrote all the time. "What does he write?" I asked curiously. "Oh, just stories," she said. "Stories he remembers from his grandparents, aunts, and uncles, some of whom had been slaves before the Civil War. He always wants me to listen to his stories, but I tell him I don't have time to listen." Now I was intrigued. I asked Teryl if her father would mind if I read the stories.

The next week, Teryl brought me a black loose-leaf binder with 150 carefully hand-written pages of clear script in black ink. In order to save paper, Arthur Mitchell had lined in between the given lines, so that each page contained about double the number of words he might have written on that page. Teryl told me that her father had worked for the Cabildo, part of the Louisiana State Museum System in New Orleans, for about 40 years. During his two 15-minute breaks each day, Arthur Mitchell would go to the 3rd floor attic of the museum, where he had a small table and chair. There he would write the stories he had heard as a young boy growing up in the French Quarter of New Orleans. According to his own account, in those days, children did not "run the streets at night," but they sat around a coal or wood-burning stove and listened to the stories told by their elders.

Some of Mitchell's immediate family had been born into slavery, or just after the Emancipation Proclamation, and their recollections illustrate the time of transition from the viewpoint of one family and small community in South Louisiana. Some of Mitchell's ancestors could read and write, and they had hidden their written stories under the floorboards, still in fear of being discovered even after all the years since their lives in slavery.

That night, I carried home what I recognized to be a very precious document, and sat down to begin reading. What I encountered electrified me. Mitchell's story began in the Lake Tanganyika region of Central Africa, detailing the customs and way of life of the people there. I was not aware of any other slave accounts that actually began in Africa, least of all in East Central Africa, describing the tribal way of life and describing an actual capture.

The narrative centers around the oldest son of one of the original captives, a beautiful young girl named Ablibobee, and her master, a French farmer named Artie (or Artee) Jons, whose plantation seems to have been located somewhere in the Tchoupitoulas region around New Orleans. Born of this union, Henry Goody Jons evidently so resembled his white father that he was offered the opportunity to pass for white and to inherit all that his father owned and could provide. Unwilling to deny his black mother and siblings, Henry Jons declined the offer and lived out his adult life as a pastor to the little black community that emerged following their release from slavery.

As I read, I was touched and amazed by the account of a captured and enslaved people who, having been previously taught and Christianized by British missionaries, struggled to live out the gospel message of love and forgiveness toward one's enemies. From the original voyage account of slaves who saved the life of their captor to the stories of being sold into slavery, I found Mitchell's "slave stories" unlike anything I had previously read. For example, these slaves, having been previously educated by British missionaries, could read and write English and do basic mathematics. These slaves were advertised all over the South at a time when few French farmers could boast of the same skills and when women running plantations on their own had need of slaves who could read and write.

Mitchell notes in his manuscript that slave-owners in New Orleans, especially, would not buy light-skinned slaves (presumably those from the Western Coast of Africa) because dark-skinned captives, once they had accepted the fact that they were slaves, were immensely loyal to and protective of their owners, although they had every opportunity they needed to poison or to kill those who owned them. People in New Orleans depended on their house slaves to shop, cook, care for their children, and manage their households. What emerges here and there in Mitchell's account is the often very close relationship that existed between the slave-owners and the slaves, especially in the city and surrounding areas. In the more outlying areas (called "parishes" in Louisiana), those relationships did not exist, as evidenced by the hatred and fear of blacks that characterized the period immediately following the Civil War.

During that time, Pastor Johns had to deal with the bickering and divisions within the Black community, as well as the destructive forces from the white community. He took on himself the burdens of both groups, making it his mission in life to show "what love could do." His mantra was, "I love people—all people."

In these pages, we find cameos of a 19th-century way of life that changed dramatically from slavery to freedom following the Emancipation Proclamation. We find a frightened and sometimes bigoted white population unsure of what the future would bring, and a Black community led by Pastor Johns, who continually taught them to love one another as well as to love those who did not love them. He himself was their example---extending his hand in welcome to all he met, regardless of race, color, or status. He taught little children to be kind to one another and he taught the Black community to forgive those who had enslaved and mistreated them. More than just words or sermons, he daily lived out his message of love and forgiveness. Toward the end of his life, he stepped between an enraged white sheriff and an innocent young Black man, saying "When you have finished listening to me, you can begin shooting."

His death brought together for the first time the entire community, white and Black. It was said of him then that he "wore love like a garment," incarnating in his own life the Christian message and thereby changing an entire community, down to the present generation.

The message passed on to Arthur Mitchell and to his cousins and siblings was more than a collection of "slave stories;" it was a clear message that hatred and resentment was a more powerful bondage than that of slavery itself. The stories preserve not so much the experience of a people in slavery, but rather of a people who preserved their core values and vision of life while in slavery, by holding onto the principles of love taught to them by the Gospel of Jesus Christ.

Editor's Note

Very much the story-teller, Mitchell's descriptions are precise and illuminative, often capturing the original *raconteur*'s nodding of the head or exuberance in relating the point. Although the story begins in the third person, with a narrator (Mitchell himself), it often slips into a first-person account, clearly repeating words he had heard directly from the source. Rarely does he indicate direct quotation or even seem to notice the transition from his own voice to that of another. Typical of an oral culture where story-telling recurs in relatively small segments, repeats, and double-backs upon itself, Arthur Mitchell's stories at first seem somewhat disconnected and disjointed, even confusing at times. However, I soon discovered that, also characteristic of an oral culture, each time the story recurs, another dimension or connection becomes apparent. It is possible that writing in 15-minute segments, Mitchell may have retold sections already written. However, the story which begins with a general and somewhat confusing overview becomes more clear and connected with each re-telling.

My first approach to the stories was to try to separate the threads and to make a logical narrative of them. Each time I tried, however, I found that I had destroyed the wonderful storytelling characteristic of the account. The more I struggled to make connect the threads of the story, the more hopeless the task seemed to grow. Finally, I shelved the document in light of my teaching and administrative duties, but I could not forget it.

After I had retired from my work at the Community College, and had re-built the house destroyed by Hurricane Katrina, I decided to retrieve the slave narratives from my files -- on January 15, 2008. As I read through the narrative once again, I saw it with fresh eyes and wondered whether its value as written, without extensive editing, might be even greater than a logical, linear, tale. This time, I decided to record the narrative as Arthur Mitchell wrote it, changing spelling only when it seemed absolutely necessary for comprehension. Mitchell, a writer who occasionally looked up words he had misspelled, characteristically reverses letters in certain words ("su" for "us," for example, and "ture" instead of "true"). As I considered these reversals—and sometimes wrong spellings---part of the charm of the narrative, and as I considered them not too distracting for the reader, I decided at first to leave them in place. Later, however, I considered that the general reader might consider the document un-edited, and so changed my mind, even while preserving my original, un-edited document for the future.

Although Mitchell completed only the fourth grade, I found his punctuation amazingly sophisticated in many places, and I reproduced it as faithfully as possible. There are places in the manuscript where it is difficult to tell whether a period or a comma was intended; in those places, I simply made a choice in favor of correctness. Many times, sentences collide with one another, as though the writer was attempting to complete a thought without realizing how it began. In those cases, for the sake of the reader, I have inserted periods between sentences. At first, I did so without capitalizing the second sentence in order to preserve Mitchell's narrative as much as possible. In preparing the book for publication, however, I soon realized that what I believed to be "charming," and "preserving the original document as closely as possible" would appear to the reader as carelessness.

My struggle was not to over-correct Mitchell's story so that it sounded more like the editor than the story-teller. In many places, I have chosen to allow expressions to remain because of their flavor rather than because of their correctness. Mitchell will most often string several (or more) sentences together, separated only by "and," thus capturing the wonderful sound of a real story. I have chosen to preserve that style throughout the book. Wherever I have felt it necessary to insert words into the manuscript for readability, I have included them in brackets [ ].

Finally, while there is some occasional indication of paragraphing and indentation in the narrative, there are pages and pages without paragraph breaks. Where the text seems to permit it, I have separated segments for the sake of readability. Although there are no chapters in Mitchell's document, I have inserted them where it seemed appropriate to do so. Only in one place does the narrative seem to have a "chapter title," which I have included here.

Since I had promised Teryl and her father that I would never publish the document without their consent, I began to try locating the Mitchell family. Finally tracking them down, I learned that Teryl had died from a wasting disease on January 15, 2007, exactly one year to the day previous to my re-discovery of the document. Her father, Arthur, had died in August of 2002. Teryl's mother, Josephine, was still living in her 9th ward home, just two miles from the levee break that wrought so much havoc in that part of New Orleans. Her home, built by Arthur himself, had been ravaged by the flood, but remained standing, even though almost everything else in the neighborhood was destroyed down to the foundations. The entire contents of the house, including Mitchell's hand-written narratives, had been carried away by the storm surge. I had in my possession the only copy of his irreplaceable stories. I knew then that it was time to bring them to light, preserving them not only for Arthur Mitchell and his family, but for all of us.

I am profoundly grateful that these papers were not lost from my possession, despite extensive damage to both the retirement home I had bought on the Mississippi Coast on August 1, 2005, and the New Orleans home I was trying to sell at the time of the storm. I am also profoundly grateful for the gracious and loving hospitality of Josephine Mitchell, Arthur's widow, who is a story all her own.

Gayle Nolan
January 15, 2012

Chapter 1

The man whose name this story bears was named at birth Henry Goody Jons after his slave owner's father, the grandson of a French immigrant whose name was Artee Jons, who was known as Master Jons. Whose mother was a captive African girl whose native name was Abli-bo-bee, bought off of the slave block at the Cabildo in New Orleans in the eighteen-twenties[1] by Mister Artee Jons of whom she beared three children for.

The first-born was named Henry Goody Jons, but after the Civil War, his father gave the whole place or slave camp to his former slaves, which had temporarily been a plantation where those people were given the house [and] land wherein they dwelled -- that became Jons Town (Village) and the church was also named the Jons Town Baptist Church. All were carrying the name "Jon" in appreciation for the kindness shown them then and long before his French wife died by falling off a horse and before he bought that beautiful little African girl and before the Civil War. So when he became the pastor of the Jons Town Baptist church, he didn't want his name "Jons" to come in conflict with the name of the church and town. Consequently, he changed the spelling of his name from Jon to Johns. The whole thing was named after the former master's grandfather's last name (family name), who came to this country on an immigrant ship along with many poor farmers from throughout Europe, but on that particular ship were three brothers with their three families who were Jon brothers. The younger brother Artee Jon, was a lawyer, but was also on the farm for lack of work in the law practice in his country. And the Jon brothers were given three hundred acres of land each, which gave them a nine-hundred-acreage of land -- well more than enough for a small town or village. It became Jons Town, which was previously a plantation converted from slavery after the Civil War, then into Jons Town. There were two other plantations, one on either side, about two hundred acre farms, combined with the Jons Town Village, which gave the town an acreage of some fourteen hundred acres.

1 Later, Mitchell writes that the first auction took place in 1810, a date I was able to verify from another source. There seem have been two auctions included in this oral history, the second in 1846.

The slaves living on the Jons Place were so free or rather almost free, so much so that slaves ran away from other places to get there; they lived in two-and three-room dwellings, with rough wood floors and a small porch in the front, whereas most other places had two rooms, no porches and dirt floors. However for some unknown reason -- for the better, or worse?-- it was said that the African girls were pretty and so nicely-built that they were almost unresistable, which may not have been the best thing for them, because of the lust mixed with the sexual greed and power, and the world-wide aspect of that day of slave owner-ship of people as a piece of property like a house, a tree, an animal or people (slaves). You may do as you please with your property when they are slaves; otherwise, they are just subjects if under a king, dictator, chief, or system.

The question is whose fault would you say slavery was in this country? There is nobody really to blame, because ever since men began to lust after what [their] neighbor has and [they get] it by warring, they found out that it was more profitable to enslave their captives rather then kill them. Now there was another form of slavery, called "servants bondage;" people were either bought or were born in bondage -- which was called servant-borns – men, born-maid, or handmaid before the New Testament of the Bible. Even Abraham was allowed by God to buy servants (slaves); slavery, bondage, servants being bought, sold, or born in, has been going on all over the world for thousands of years. There were some white slaves, but hardly captives -- mostly those poor whites who couldn't make it would sell themselves into slavery, because the owners were afraid to buy light-skinned captive as slaves.

The traders of slaves had to take their light-skinned slaves to another country to sell because the owners said they could trust or turn their backs, or go to sleep, trust babies with [the darker-skinned slaves][2] and eat their cooking, and because they [the darker-skinned slaves] are physically stronger [from] their excessive exercise and their outdoor jungle-type living, hard work, hunting without guns, training for tribal warfare and animal attacks on them. It is commonly said that as a rule, men grow larger and stronger in the outdoor rugged life, and where there is a continual dangerous situation which makes them keep in mind they may have to fight off some self - made greedy renegade tribal people or wild hateful beast, snake, or hateful bird. There are a number of long large snakes all around and through the land; that's why they must keep their eyes open and their senses keen. They were taught to fight all creatures with the idea of either kill or be killed,

---

2 My insertion, based on later information in the document.

even if it is a spider or some kind of bug. They knew from small boys that they were going to have to be men among men, and they grew up into full manhood. It was imperative that all of the young men keep buried in their minds that they must be ready at all times to protect your women, children, and old folks at the risk of your own life.

So here we have it, in of all places primitive Africa, they knew way back there [about] exercise and mind training by force of survival, for they knew [about] the working of the mind toward being man enough and tough enough to take on anything from an ant to an elephant. In their minds they believed so strongly that they actually had mind-eyes in back of them. They said many times they would turn in a split second before being hit, or attacked by animals or snakes that may fall out of a tree on someone. And now in these late times, we are bragging about mind power, and mind control, which we believe never fails, wherein way back there in so called "uncivilized" all- black people continent --- I can readily accept the fact that they were primitive, but not uncivilized nor a barbarous people, then or now --- in that they were able to unconsciously use mind power and mind-control to the greatest extent even as hypnosis, magic, witchcraft, and voo-doo, which is still common in the United States today. We brag a lot about positive thinking just as they did back there.

In Africa, they said they had a few magicians, and herb doctors, and a host of different kinds of herb medicines. They kept themselves clean out of necessity because they lived so close to the ground. The female had to be especially clean and careful because she had the whole family's health in her hands. And young girls watched their mothers to learn about life because they gloried in coming into ladyhood so as to become wives and mothers, even as most of the young girls around the world during their youth from time to time think about motherhood.

Now this beautiful young girl, along with a number of other African people, was kidnapped from her native land, but this girl in particular after being bought as a slave, was actually a wife and mother of her so-called slave master, a French man named Artee Jons, the son of a French immigrant who bought an African captive girl off a slave auction block in New Orleans, whose native name was Ablibobee. She gave birth to three children for him. The first-born was a boy, who was named Henry Goody Jons. Jons was the French name of his biological father. He -- Henry Goody Jons -- asked his paw to let him change the spelling of his last name because he did not want his name to be the same as the town and Church of our thankful dwelling place: "I am not now nor will I ever be good

3

enough for the name of this town and Church. Let me change it from Jons to Johns." He said, reluctantly, "alright." Of course, this did not occur until such time as he became the pastor of the Jons Town Baptist Church. And from that day, until the day he died, he was known as Pastor Johns to the colored, white, and non-white, about all of whom he has said or had been heard saying, "I love you as if you were me, and that is whether you love me or not. You see I love you because you are people and I love people: all people. These are the words of our Lord Jesus Christ, who says, 'Love one another as I loved you, or as yourself.' You are supposed to love everybody: rich people, the poor, the sick, the well, the white people, colored people, red people, tan people, yellow people, and if there be any other color of people, you supposed to love them too as you love yourself."

Pastor John's mother changed her name from her native African name Ablibobee to an American name Clamentine Jons; her native name Ablibobee was some what difficult for Americans to pronounce. These were the names of the three children she had for her slave master Artee Jons; the first born was Henry Goody Jons; the second child was a girl who they named Johnnean. The third was a boy they named Hardy Jons. It was said that their mother was a very beautiful, graceful, and kind person. She was one of the sixty people brought to New Orleans to be sold into slavery. Slavery? Yes it was a very common phenomenon all over the world in those days.

Those people were captured from somewhere in east central Africa along the Tanganyika Lake, where there was a lot of fresh water which was about the largest fresh water supply in all of Africa. There are a few rivers not too far away; they ever so often dried up during very hot months, but the lake is so long and very deep that it never goes dry, as far as we know, which gave them a large fresh water supply for drinking and fishing. Many eastern African tribes had situated themselves along the Lake because of the host of small and rather large fish, where men and boys did a whole lot of fishing, mostly at night, in their own built dug-out boats by cutting down very big -around trees, and somehow they found a way to split those trees in two, then did whatever it took to dig out and shape that half-log into a boat. Each boat was shaped and styled by their individual liking; every man styled his different from all of the other boats among them, however long it took. They built those boats anywhere from ten-to-twenty feet long, and about ten feet wide. They would cut, shape, and style with all their hearts insomuch that each person of the family, young and old, recognized their boat on sight because of the style wherein they were built.

And these boats were passed down from father to son. However, they had to be very careful not to dig too deep, or too wide, into the sides of it. They said building a boat was like bringing up a child: once it gets started, you can't stop until it is grown.

They didn't think that Lake was navigable for any larger boats or ships until such time as they were being invaded. Seeing one morning a large white boat almost as big as a ship, pulling up or drifting toward their banks, they were rather glad to see the boat. They thought it to be the returning British Christian missionaries coming back to teach them more about that Great Messiah, the Lord Jesu Christ, which has already come. Of whom the Jews had been there previously teaching them that the Messiah was coming soon; they were going everywhere they could teaching Judaism. They had been half-way around the world trying to make Jewish Proselytes; which means people converted to Judaism or becoming Jews. However, by then the Christian missionaries were turning the world upside down for Jesus Christ. This was one of the larger tribes living along the Lake here which had been converted to Christ already for a number of years, and most of them had learned to read and write and some mathematics, and how to speak good English -- all of this the British missionaries taught them. Howbeit they by necessity would go home during the winter raining season during which time there was an almost everyday rain. And they would surely return after two or three months. And when they came back, they would bring all kinds of goodies, toys, sweets, books, writing paper, and a lot of used clothes and shoes, and of course some medicine for their brothers and sisters in Christ. When they did come back, they came in much smaller boats, going up and down the Lake area trying to covert as many tribes, whole tribes as possible, but they could only go to the people who were not hostile toward Christians and Jews, such as the Islamic, M [uslim],3 and a few others, all of which are religious beliefs. Most of them had their own belief about religion, God, heaven, and hell. The Christians are said to be the only religious belief who does not dislike people of other beliefs; even the roman church does not believe in, nor perform, nor teach the aspects of their Bible: and they are world wide, so what?

They were one of the Christian tribes having learned how to love one another by the teaching of the Bible, mostly the Gospel of Christ, which made them so much more humane toward each other owing to their

---

3 My insertion. Mitchell wrote only "M."

newfound knowledge of the almighty God -- as you will hear later on in this story, Pastor Johns saying such things as this. Whether you believe it or not, there is something you must admit -- that there is some adhesive power in Christianity, in that, if you take hold of it, it will _____4 to you, not turn loose until you die, because Christianity is just running over with that Great Giant and uncontrollable monstrous beast, the untamable killer serpent; yet it's sweeter [than] honey -- that great wonderful thing we call love! It has more power than all the armies on earth put together into one, with all of their modern weapons, yet love is still the greatest real true power ever since day one. It is the only thing that has the power to make people free even though still in bondage, because it is impossible to enslave the mind.

Although some people had to die in that Tanganyika area invasion-type kidnapping, it had been said by some of the captives that leaving [their] native land was like getting out of prison. And some of the freed slaves after the Civil War had been heard saying that this whole aspect of being brought to this country has been proven to have been a blessing in disguise. Sometimes they laugh about how this thing actually happened. It was really a great surprise to all of us: it was about time for the missionaries to return and we were looking for them any day but those men got off the boat with guns rather than hymn books and Bibles. We knew about guns because a few of the tribes had them. Now the invasion was done [in this way]. When those men put their foot on the ground, they started shooting, rounding up in a huddle. They shot a couple of old men, but when the young people saw what was going on, not knowing the danger of guns yet, they took to the woods, and once they were in the woods, that was the end of it. It was no use going after them, because they had been taught how to keep trees between themselves and their pursuer. The only children who didn't get away were the ones who wanted to stay with their parents. The boat's men did not shoot at the children and young people who ran into the wood also. But they were still able to gather twenty children, and twenty-two young girls, and about eighteen young men, and two whole families, to be sold to some rich old folks who just needed to have other people in the house with them and maybe a few young people around, sometimes as house keepers, and other times just [for] companionship.

In this invasion, there was a girl so very beautiful being kidnapped. She was so pretty and well-built that the boat captain asked her name; she

---

4 Occasionally there are gaps in the document. I assume that Mitchell intended to return later to fill them in.

said my name is Ablibobee. She looked so good that she was sold for a very handsome price [and] later became the mother of Henry Goody Jons, who was later known as Pastor Johns.

The boat came back to New Orleans in the Mississippi River and Bienville Street Ramp in the New Orleans French Quarters -- the camp at Bienville and the river, where the superdome was [later] built. The ramp was where the slaves debarked, which was the most convenient because the boat would come in [when] the tide was high, and drift out when the tide was low. They would unload and wait for the Tide to _____and would just drift out. It was a good place to load or unload because of the great downward ramp where all of those who survived the trip would debark and walk to the New Orleans Cabildo.

Of course, many of those captives choose death rather than slavery by refusing to eat or drink anything; you just can't make a person do anything short of death. Some even jumped overboard in open seas with little or no hope of survival, saying, "I would rather die than live in bondage." The rest of them did survive the trip and were customarily walked to the New Orleans Cabildo from the boat, which was about five blocks. The Cabildo -- this is where Louisiana Purchase was signed in the year of Lord eighteen o three, and that table and chairs are still there, in that same room, in the same place where it was at the signing thereof, and the original slave auction block, which was nothing but a round block of wood cut from the bottom of a very large tree and it was placed on the ground in the courtyard of the Cabildo, where I saw [it] in the nineteen sixties, during the time it had to be removed from the rear yard, where there was a yard with extremely high walls around the whole place, walls high and thick. And there were a number of jail-type cells that the traders of incoming slaves would use as a place of store house, wherein they would store their human cargo until such time as the auction did take place. These cells measured about twelve-by-twenty feet, with brick and clay floors, and no windows...one big door with an opening about five-by-seven, built with planks about an inch-and-a-half-thick by four-to-ten-inches wide, to about seven feet high, with a rather unique type of iron bars fixed on the outside of those big thick doors, and on those large iron bars were very large brass padlocks. Now I don't know where that slave block was originally placed, but when I saw it, it was fixed in front of those cells. You may have heard the very old rumor that New Orleans in those days was the center of the slave trade throughout the whole deep south.

So, then the time had come to auction off their human cargo of men, women, children, and families, the news had already covered the whole south. The news said, *We have what we think to be the last boatload of black African slaves who are somewhat intelligent.* Of course slave traders would buy, sell, or ____ people of any race or color, and any young age, any where, and anyway they could get people to sell. However, this meant kidnap, trickery, gimmicks, or such snatching of any person if not too old. The light-skinned captives had no buyers in the United States, so they were reluctant to bring them into the southern United States because they would only buy the Africans, but they must be black Africans. I had been taught all of [my] life that Africa was the largest continent on earth, and I had been told all of [my] life that all of the inhabitants of Africa were black, and that is not true. The owners found out that once the Africans found themselves in bondage, they could be trusted, and that they just would not murder anybody -- yet they had all of the opportunities to kill if they were killers. They surely could have poisoned them; many of them could have been strangled to death, or just beaten to death. Of course the whites could be sold in some other countries such as in Europe and other parts of the world. They [were] to be used in different homes and positions, like bus boys, butlers, maids, nursing, care of old people, housekeepers, governess, care for horses, work on farms, milk cows, dig and repair wells and outhouses, work on roads, keep fences, and many other things.

When they came for that auction, they were ready to buy all of these twenty-two young African girls, to be put up for bid, and eighteen young muscular men, and that brought a lot of men and women -- all rich people. When the women wanted some person, they would not be outbid, plus a few old folks looking for families having mother, father, and children for housekeepers and/or companionship. Some of these people were rather old and alone, whose family had died or just took off and forgot about them; many slaves in New Orleans were willed their freedom by inheriting it. We don't know much about that, except that somehow they could not own an estate or a large tract of land. New Orleans history backs this up.

The auction was held about the first day of June in the year of Our Lord eighteen-ten; this auction did take place in the courtyard of the New Orleans Cabildo next door to the Saint Louis Cathedral, one of the older Catholic Churches in the United States, in what is said to be the queen city of the south. Most of those African girls who were bought off the slave block did, or most likely, wind up mistresses and mothers of their owners' children, but those old folks who told us all of those what I believe to be true stories told us that most of those Tanganyika area slaves were not black *per se*, but their skin complexion was sort of tan -- like falling leaves. When I say black, I am thinking of tar; when I say white, I think of snow. Their hair was somewhat kinky but soft and controllable. Their skin was rather oily, owing to the fact that they ate a lot of coconuts, fish, and a lot of other kinds of nuts, all of which had a heavy oil content. They say that dry skin may crack.. The women were not very tall, not more than five-feet, seven-inches tall, and none of them were fat. Well, the men were rather tall and large, and none were fat nor short but necessarily muscular and big enough and strong enough and quick enough to survive under those tribal jungle wildwood conditions, where they may have to fight off anything, because from a little boy they had to be taught about the constant danger of warfare by some other tribe, and teaching, _____be over-run your tribe, your enemies will kill your old folks, and take your young men captive, enslaving some of them, and holding the rest of them to be sold to slave traders into slavery. Your children will be given to whoever wanted or needed them to become their own children. Your young women will be sold to the warriors as rewards, and all of the rest of the captives into a stockade to await the traders, to be sold to them.

Most of the boys, almost all of the boys, at just about babies had to begin training for their whole tribal survival, and they would never stop that training until they were men. Despite all of that training, they were no match for guns. These people were said to be the Aeciagogoa Tribe, named after their ancient founder, one of the native tribes of the Tanganyika area. To them, their women were vastly beautiful, and they were willing to protect them with the last drop of their blood, and the same thing went for their old folks and children. They had very smooth skin and they did not get fat nor tall, but they bragged abut their legs and their small br----- maybe their diet had something to do with that, which consisted of a lot of cused and some wild meat, a lot of their own-grown vegetables, and all of wild leaves and vegetables and fruits; they ate as much as they could find in the woods. It was in abundance, [and] this food was full of iron, oils, and vitamins. Those old folk told us that such things as beans and potatoes, mostly sweet potatoes, would literally grow under their feet; they believed [it] did show in their bodies and skin. Howbeit the auction did go on as planned, on the first day of June eighteen-ten, about ten a.m.

Now the rich white men and women that came were not a few. I say that because there were some free colored people living in New Orleans at that time, but they did not come to auctions even though free, but [they were] not allowed to own, buy, or sell slaves. They were nevertheless free, but when one group of persons are not free in a nation, the whole nation is in bondage. They were free, but not equal. We know only what those old former slaves used to tell us about the things they knew about and [had] actually seen and heard during their time in slavery, and some of the people were able to buy their freedom or rather, someone buys their freedom for them, or some had just been given or awarded, or, in some cases, their freedom was obtained by being legally willed to them.

Some of the white women could not or would not have children but still had an affection for them, and would like to have a few of them around and had enough money to buy some at the auction where the boys were the first to go on the auction block first to be sold to the highest bidder, and they were quickly sold for a very good price, up to more than a hundred dollars each, for the boys and a little less for the girls. After all of the children were sold, then they put up these young muscular men, (buyers called [them] boys), all of whom were bought by the women. The bidding took a little longer for one reason. This auction was for more than just buying men for their workability, but these men were educated; they could read, write, do mathematics, and speak good English. Some of the owners needed people who could read and write, because some of them could not, among the men and women. The bidding was very sharp, but those rich women would not be outbid; consequently the women bought all eighteen of those men at an incredible price.

Those rich women bought those male slaves because they had need for men, or a man around their estate, some of them whose husbands were disabled, or dead, or just took off, but the dwelling still remained, and all of its duties that needed to be done by some man, things that women ought not to think of doing, such as driving horse and carriages, or wagons, small or large wagons, teams, keep down weeds, and grass cut down, drive and care for livestock, repairing fences, watch closely over the wells and out-houses, and dig new ones when necessary, to cut down trees, cut them up and haul back as firewood and fence posts, bringing inside the firewood, when the weather is cold, to keep enough firewood near the fireplace at all times, and a few logs when raining cold nights to burn all day, and all night. That was done as a part of a male slave's duty to his mistress -- to see to it that his madam, which all women slave owners were called by their slaves, had warmth in her bed all night, and do whatever he could to be sure that she was comfortable and satisfied before she would give him permission to leave her house and go to his dwelling.

The Africans were not known to be murderers -- not that they never killed, but kill and murder are not the same. But in the United States they did kill, but only when they were pushed too far before they would decide [to] kill and take to the woods, and once in the woods, that was it. One of those old former New Orleans slaves told us that some of their men had hands so big that they could choke a man to death with one hand.

One old lady (white) told us what [are] called true living stories that they think will never die, and at one moment, the old soul just stood up and put one hand on her hip and moved a little and said, "Children, as a rule, people like to get what they pay for, even when buying slaves, and when they bought us, the men and the women, they got what they paid for and a hell of a lot more." And we almost fell out laughing at that.

The selling of those men and children took that whole day, but that was most important, because there were twenty-two young east central African Girls [that] would be sold. None of those girls were more than thirteen years old. Educated African people were somewhat unheard of in those times, but those African people had been taught from little children, and still are being taught general education and English by the British missionaries, which "...if they [the missionaries] were there during the time of that invasion, we would [have] had to kill them as a cover up, but who would have had to bear that blame for the lives of those people? Nobody could make England believe anything else." The auctioneer said all of that to say that [this] was their last voyage anywhere seeking human cargo. "We know that when England hears about this, and they will, they will surely send some troops in that area to protect their missionaries." He went on to say, "If we don't get a satisfactory bid for these little nigger girls, we will not sell them today at all."

So they brought them up one at a time, and placed them on the slave block. The girls were purposely slightly dressed, with a piece of cotton cloth around their waist, and just enough to meet around the waist, and about eleven inches long, with nothing on else on and of course topless. To some of the older owners, those young virgin Africans [were] nothing but children; little girls were referred to as Black. On this day, the Auctioneer said he would not entertain any bid under one hundred dollars for each girl. One man bid one hundred one dollars, which kept going up all the way to about two hundred dollars, and some of them were sold for much more, as high as three hundred or more dollars:

Now there was one of those girls they held back until last, whose African native name was Ablibobee, because she was so beautiful. There had been rumors concerning her. When they had sold all of the other girls, then the Auctioneer stepped up on the block and said, exclaiming, "Gentlemen! Here is that beautiful little East Central African Nigger Girl! She is the prettiest little thing I have ever seen! Yes sir! Just look at her: she's got everything, body and all. Well, here she is boys!"

And when they saw her, they almost panicked, saying one thing and then another about her whole body, showing their anticipations of lust in the action and voice, pushing and shoving in their trying to outbid each other, starting at three hundred dollars, going up to almost five hundred dollars. Than a rich Frenchmen came up, whose wife died two years previously by falling off of a horse. He said to [the] Auctioneer, "Sir, I bid seven hundred dollars." The Auctioneer said, "Mister Artee, what did you say?" He replied, "I will give seven hundred dollars for that little Nigger Girl; will anybody pay more?" When no one said anything, the Auctioneer said, "Sold to Mister Artee Jons!" He walked up and took off his shirt and wrapped it around her. He winked at her and they were both smiling with each other walking to his carriage. Then he picked her up and placed her in his carriage, and they took off to what became her home, as a wife and mother, until her death. Artee Jons was her slave master, and the father of her children, for she gave birth to three children of him, two boys and one girl. Her first-born was a boy who they named Henry Goody Jons; the second child was a girl, whose name was Johnnian Jons; and the third child was a boy named Hardien Jons. These were the three children of the so-said, the most beautiful African girl, who was the mother of the man who was known as Pastor Johns. Her native name was Ablibobee. Henry, the first boy, was born almost like an identical _____ of his French father, who he called "Paw." And this was in just about every respect: his paw was a lawyer; he looked so much like his father that his paw wanted to declare him a white person, telling him how easy it would be for him in that he had everything he needed to do so, to go all the way to the white house, and all three of his children had a very good home education, but he still refused to be white knowing the many advantages in being a white person. But he still chose to be colored, which was said to be rather common in those days for mulattos (half whites) who could have passed as white folks but would not, just like Pastor Jons did, because some of them, like Johns, had darker mothers, brothers, and sisters whom they loved very much, lots too much to discriminate against them. However, the Jons family was a closely knit family in a Godly type love of undying quality that stuck out all over them. And that was all of them -- their French father, African mother, brothers, and sister.

Their mulatto children were reared with good morals, and good manners, and a deep-rooted Christian faith. They knew in those days [that] if they passed as white folks, that they were going to have to act the part, and that might make changes in their whole way of thinking. No more "love ye one another," no more mixing with dark-skinned people, not even their own mother and them. They [would] have to teach their children they are better, and are more intelligent and superior and serve a different God than colored people, and that's the reason their skin is not dark, and their hair is not kinky, and many inhuman teachings. The bad thing about the wrong kind of training, or teaching, [is that] some of those children will never learn any better, or the truth, and some never want [to] know the truth, and never do until it's much too late, when sickness, pains, diseases, accidents, mental or physical problems, trouble with love or loved ones, trouble coming, coming before they knew about it. All of this and a lot more -- [people] try to tell you better, but to no avail, because whatever a person is taught from a baby to their fifteen-to-twenty years of their life by words and/or example, somehow becomes in most cases a part of that person, as much as any of your body parts. For an example, I was from a small child [taught] that hate for any people was satanic. [It was] satanic seventy years ago, and I still believe that hate is the practice of Satanism, and if a person can believe in [his] heart that only God is supreme with superior power, I believe that person is wise. This may not have been a true p_____ of the fact, but it was commonly believed among most of the colored people, that vast majority of mulattos (half white) who passed as white folks was only for opportunity, such as equal change, freedom of movement, and most of all: Justice before the Law, and of course----Jobs, and whatever.

Now this was the second time that a boat left New Orleans with the intent to obtain slaves by an invasion-type kidnapping, when previously they would just take their voyage knowing that there were captive people to be sold to any buyer, but since England had outlawed the buying [and] selling of slaves, and Northern United States did the same, made the captives for sale very scarce.

So the Auctioneer said to the people, "This time we are going out of the ship- and boat-building business, and no slave trading at all. However, we have a boat-load of the most wonderful captives on this Auction ever— all special people who are so unique that if we could have, we would have brought them back to their native land, but that would be utterly impossible and plain suicide; that's how special they are. And the boats and ship that we have are all sea going v[essels], to be sold at an action in a day or two, at [our] shipyard." This brought more than two hundred men and women of the whole south land, and these were business people who knew what they were looking for, and had already assembled themselves in the Cabildo, where the auctions were frequently held, on the last day of May at ten a.m, in the year of our Lord, eighteen-forty-six in the Cabildo in New Orleans, Louisiana. The bidding didn't actually start until twelve noon, and it was done on this wise. They put the men up first, after a couple hours [of] the men, then they put the children on the block and auctioned them off one-by-one until they were all sold to people who came for the chance to buy a few kids. There were also a few rich old folks there looking for small families, such as father, mother, and a few children; they did bring the families up and was sold after a lot of bidding, because those old folks would [not] be outbid, but those old owners, mostly older men with wives, and sometimes families, they didn't care about that. Those slaves were really nothing but children (little girls) but the white women, when first married were young, nice-looking, thin, small waistline, smooth skin and a lot of life in them, but time has a way of changing things, just about all things! Well, here [we] have little girls that those old men could buy, and a wife past thirty years old, [who] has began to look a little old, getting a little fat, a few wrinkles showing up around their mouth, eyes, neck and general body. Those old owners had another way of getting younger women, and this is the last boat load of slaves coming to New Orleans, as far as they knew, so they [were] very nervous waiting for those young girls to [go] on that auction block. The time did come when they put them on the block one at a time, very scarcely dressed. When their lustful eyes saw them, they started bidding, and almost bid the shirts off of their backs.

After all that was over, the Auctioneer started telling about his special captive family, but first he said that this was his last voyage to Africa or anywhere else seeking human cargo. The Auctioneer was actually the captain of the boat which [was] owned by his father. And all of the money from this trip, and half of all the money from the selling of our ship-building business will be given to the families of those six boat's men who lost their lives on this trip---they applauded. Also the captain lost half of his right arm on that trip: "If it had not been for the boat drifting too far from land [for] the tribesmen to swim back to land safely if they were forced to jump over, [we] were far out-numbered, they only had three more to kill. I would have bled to death anyway, but the thing that saved my life, thanks be to God, there was a captive family on that boat who were herb doctors (not witch doctors) and they were very nice and kind people whose knowledge of herb medicine has trickled down to them from generation to generation for thousands of years. During the fighting between us and the tribesmen, [we] discharged our guns, [but] they kept coming at us, and the bottom part of my right arm was badly cut, broken, and hanging. Then I asked one of my boat's men if he would go down in the hold of the boat where all of the captives were, asking if anybody could and would help me with my badly cut arm. One family said they would try to do whatever they could for [me] under God." He was inquiring reluctantly if anybody knew any thing about medicine.

"That family came up whose name was the Niaconigogoa. The first thing he said [was], 'That bottom part of the arm must come off.' His wife's first name was Magania, with two girls, one eight years old. The other girl [was] just over one year old. His wife said, 'Yes we can help you. If you will stop the boat as close as you can to the land, me and my little girl will swim in and get as much as we can of the herb-medicine we need for this job, and we will come again to the boat. While we are gone my husband will be here doing whatever he can until we get back with the stuff he needs to work with on that arm of a part must come off'."

They [were] used to working on men, women, and children who had from time to time been torn by animals, snakes, and tribesmen in warfare, who sometimes tear people almost apart. Even though part of the arm had to come off, but not until his folks get back, he said. So the boat quickly drifted with care near the bank, but not too close to land so the mother and little girl had to swim about a hundred feet to land. The three surviving boat men and little girl told this story because she was that little girl, and the people believed her because the story was true! The mother and daughter placed a knife in their mouth between their teeth before entering the water. By then the captain was completely unconscious through the tribesmen hypnosis. In about three hours, the little eight year old girl and her mother swam back to the boat with large bags of stuff, such as leaves, roots, vines, bugs, insects, and skins of even snakes, all of which constituted the herb-medicine. They had been known to have said, "Even though the herbs are good, and very good, the cure really comes from the most high almighty God throughout and your faith therein, and the power of the mind which helps the body's organisms do their healing job."

They were in the woods more than two hours looking for the right herbs; even wild honey was needed to be used as an antiseptic. They even took advantage of the salt in the sea water. The thing about it was that they knew how to use every thing that they had gathered. The captain was telling this true story to those people before the boat and ship and the whole business went up for auction. He said, "So I lost part of my right arm. And no doctor on earth could have done a better job," holding his arm up, saying, "Look at it. What do you think?

"When I arrived back in New Orleans, while I was convalescing, I had a lot of time to think about all of the hurt, pain, suffering, and death that I caused, mostly out of greed. Six of my boatmen -- but I don't know how many were killed among the African tribesmen because they took their dead with them when they left off the boat. If the boat wouldn't have kept moving out from land, getting too far for them to swim back, they would have killed all of us, but just the thought of how wonderful, helpful, and kind that doctor's family was to me, after kidnapping them to be sold as common cargo. It made feel like a sick dog."

Chapter 2

I used to just love to be around those old folks, listening to them telling those beautiful, yet a little bitter sometimes, stories from the slavery past, that will always be a part of them, and will follow them like time. Their words to us were like reading a history book.

They told us about the captain who lost half of his right arm on his last voyage to Africa on his father's boat, who had until then owned a small ship-and boat - building business; their family name was Loranzin. The older son [was] Jonia Jontontia. The other son's name was Wisedena Jontontia. *(marginal note: older. Montana/ young. Loranzine)*[5] Their mother died with tuberculosis. Their paw went hunting in the wood behind their house and was (not) seen. Jonia just was not around any more. The people knew that they did dispute over house, land, money and slave-ownership, and all Mon[tana's] friends began to ask about him. Wisedena would say, "Oh he was worrying so much over paw, and nearin' death, he just sold out to me and went to the big city," but they knew he was lying, that [he] had killed all of them, even though the family was Christians, but he did not believe in God at all, and made it known how he felt about God, heaven, and hell also the hereafter.

Wisedena, the young son was about forty years old when the last of his family was gone. Whatever happened to them, then he owned everything -- the house, money, land, and the slaves -- and that's what [he] wanted, to be called Master Loranzine. And within a week, he had given out an order that he must be referred to at all times by every body as "Master Loranzine." When the old man supposedly died in the woods, it was three days before he claimed to have found him and buried him. But the friends and neighbors of Montana knew that he was dead, because he only had one arm and was rather friendly with the neighbors, but had little say around the farm, and just about everything else. That caused a lot of dispute over houses, land, money, and the old man's slaves, even the livestock. After Montana had not been seen or heard from for more than a month, more people were inquiring about his whereabouts. His younger brother would

5 This note is part of the original text; Mitchell occasionally makes marginal notes as if he needed to ascertain or maybe later recall specifics.

say the same thing:"He decided to go, and sold me his whole share of everything, and he took off with just about all of the cash money, and every bit of the jewelry, all the gold, and left," but nobody believed him about his brother, nor his paw. He really tried to put the bluff, saying he was so worried about his parent's death, he thought it better to leave the house. His mother died with tuberculosis which was commonly known as TB.

Now that all the slaves belonged to him that lived in his slave village where the white and colored slaves lived together, and under the same conditions, Loranzine Jontontia preferred to be called by his first name Loranzine, and be known as "Master Loranzine" and "Sir." Then he put on a new form of power to be used as a devil dressed up in human flesh, a most Godless person. Even though his parent and older brother were very religious, he was an infidel. He began to rule with an iron hand so quickly, which made the people believe all the more that he killed both his paw and brother for greed and power. He went to a Mississippi slave-camp where they enslave all kinds of animals like horses, cows, mules, and men and women, and dogs for sale; he bought two white families – slaves, that is -- sold for any reason you want them, for these people were so poor that they had been sold to the slave camp. It was said this camp would buy any animal or person of any [color or race] up to thirty years old. In that camp, they treated those people like dirt. And when Master Loranzine bought them, they were so poor, hungry, uneducated, and backward, he actually treated them [like] thrown - away trash. He gave them one corn-shuck mattresses for each family. A man named Ben Gumine said he and some of the other men showed them how to build themselves beds, chairs, and tables, because they had to live with the Negro slaves, which was common practice.

Most white people or families who were in slavery were those who for some reason had borrowed money from [a] wealthy family who would seize their own mother's property for lack of payment, so when they could not make payment to the lender, the lender had the legal rights to confiscate everything that family had, even the family. In some cases they did, but mostly voluntary done. They just placed themselves in bondage rather than see their family starve to death. Even though they had land, [they] owed more on it than they were able to pay. Some poor people had no choice because of age, sickness, or just being disabled but to go into bondage; some just would take off from the south.

He went back to Mississippi to buy two men. Those two men were so dumb and weak - minded that he made them his executioners. Their job was to slay anybody that their Master Loranzine did not like, or got in his way, or bucked him in any way. He had been married about ten years to old man Gunburg's daughter, but they got along bad because she could not have children or would not. The slave owners, at least some of them, thought they were kings and tried to act like one, but now some of the men slaves had begun running away through the swamp land. The time had come when people would just disappear. They just wasn't seen anymore; it was commonly believed that he [killed] his paw and brother, because, as they put it, he was an Atheist.

Loranzine was born with an incurable disease which should have brought him to an early death, but because of that herb doctor African's family who knew about this disease, because it was a African jungle disease, they did heal him. This was the Nicongogoa family who changed their native names to more American type names; they made their family name Black, Lakemen Black. His wife's name [was] Fanny Black. The baby's name [was] Dolly; the older girl's name, Tanga Black. They knew what herbs and roots they needed for the cure of their master's illness -- and for anyone else who can stop hating long enough to ask for help. He had something that caused him to get an uncontrollable fit which would last sometimes for hours, but within a couple of years it was not cured, but less frequent and a little better controlled. Many people who knew him and how low-down and evil he was thought his condition was the visitation of an evil spirit, but his problem was mostly physical.

The Black family was able to help a lot of people because of the vast knowledge that they brought with or in them from the African jungles. However, it was publicly said of Miss Tanga that she was not a racial-type person, but she was color blind, and seemed to love all people. But her paw had a hang-up with the difficulty of trying to understand the -- as he called it -- the unnecessary racial and nationality hate. He said, "I am glad that in the country from whence I came, or rather the tribe I belonged to, never learned to hate. Then he asked the question, "How can any people hate another people simply because of the way they were born -- something they had absolutely nothing whatsoever to do with -- how or where they were born nor the complexions of their skin?"

If you can remember, this Tanga Black [was] the little eight-year-old girl captive in an invasion kidnapping of their father, mother, and baby sister along the Tanganyika Lake some where in East Central Africa, who swam one hundred feet from their captive boat to the land to get herbs to help the captain's wounded arm. They were brought to this country to be sold into slavery. Tanga Black, who was later known as "Miss Black," her and her mother who were on that boat and knew how she and her parents tried so hard to get those few people to eat and drink, who chose to die at sea rather live in bondage by refusing to eat, they did help a few people, but some would not eat. About ten of them did die and were thrown overboard. [They] said they would rather die being free than to live in slavery. The last words of some of those ten men and women who died for lack of food said that the fish [could] eat our flesh [rather] than to let it be used in slavery. She said that while on voyage we were not dogged and we were well fed and given good clean drinking water. And not one of the women (girls) were touched nor any attempt made upon them. "My [ ] just could not get [ ] to drink or eat anything at all. The boat's-men also tried, but to no avail, but most of us did survive the voyage."

Tanga made twelve years old, and they said she was the prettiest little thing on earth. She was so beautiful that people used to stop her on the road and say to her, "Little [girl], why are you so good-looking? What did you do to yourself?" All I could say, "I don't know; I have done nothing." She had such a nice way of walking, not sexy, but just nice and lady-like.

Now this satanic-mind slave-owner who was known as Master Loranzine, even though he had a wife, she had come to understand that her being a wife was only on paper now that he is a master, because she had no say-so at all, but like most of the slave owners' wives, she was slowly becoming somewhat like a domesticated animal, and they knew to buck them was almost surely to be fatal. The white woman wanted to, and should have been, a free person, but not in the south, where the colored woman and the white man did as they pleased, but the colored man and the white woman [were] under heavy bondage. And it [was] said when a girl got married, it was [an] abomination for her to return to her father's house. If it [is]true, it is very sad, that in many cases before those white girls would go back home in humiliation, to be scorned by her brothers and sisters, and maybe the neighbors, some wind up killing themselves, and sometime it is done for them. This man was a sexual maniac and used his power to promote his sexual greed; he had the authority and used it to run over the young slave girls. In complete disregard for his wife, he would command those girls to move into his house as maids but she knew what was going on with those girls. This was common among slave-camps, especially the owners who were not Christians, or infidels, as their Master Loranzine was, and his wife had become a victim of those times when women in the slave-camp white-woman-wife relationship where at [ ] years of age they [were] considered an old woman. There had already been three young girls in his house who had given birth to some seven children for him. Two of those girls were colored, and one of them Spanish, thirteen years old. She gave birth to two girls for him. They had no choice in the matter, because slaves all over the world were technically the property of their owner like a horse, cow, tree, or whatever.

So he sent his two, as the people called them, "slayers" for the [cute?] little girl, Tanga Black. Her parent was reluctant to let her go, but the little girl knew the pitiful consequences of refusing to obey the command of any master or king in a tribe, even a chief. The Spanish girl's paw was very sickly, and they were in great need of all their necessities; being nothing but a child, [she] really offered herself to him, knowing about his sex greed, and their need, and she had two children, both girls, but they looked too much like her family. Her name was Maixcy; she had been sent back home not long before he sent for Tanga Black. After she had a long talk with her parent, she asked the two men if they would please come back tomorrow for her; she said, "I will be ready to go when you come." She was very young, only twelve years old, but she was smart enough to know that if her parents] did not let her go, there would be some kind [of] reprisal, so in the meantime she took time to explain her feeling about the whole mess; her parents just sat down and listened: She said to them, "Morn, Paw, you know I love you, and want you alive, and I know you truly love me and want me living, right? And you saw those two men that he sent for me. If you don't let me go, [they] will be the same two dogs he will use to destroy you both. Can the subjects refuse to obey their king? No, not if they want to live; so is it here. We are owned; we are slaves; do you understand, Paw, Morn?" They nodded their heads. She went on saying, "You know what Dolly told me the other day? Being a little sad, she came over to where I was plaiting strings of garlic. I didn't know I was crying, and if I was crying, I didn't know what I was crying about. She said, 'Big sis, don't cry; some day you will be free.' I said to her, 'Little girl, how do you know?' She replied, 'You just wait and see.' I was trying to talk to her, but she went and picked up a rock. Just at the time, the ducks had start flying out of the creek to go into the woods; she pitched a rock at them, and two of the ducks fell at her feet dead. Now Paw- Morn, you know that that is impossible, don't you? Paw didn't ask her where she got them." Tanga's mother said, "I don't know how she did it; but I stewed them down with some dry rice and brown gravy and it was mighty good." Tanga said in deep wonder, "That little girl is only five years old and how can she...." Their mother stopped Tanga by placing her hand over Tanga's mouth, looking up toward heaven saying, "Lord I thank you for both of them." The family really didn't know that Dolly was a chosen individual vessel, a sacrifice of God, but it was not altogether hidden from her mother.

Well, it was about time for Tanga to start getting ready and a few things to think about before he[r] departure tomorrow morning, not knowing how long she would be gone, but she thought it would [not] be any longer than the time he sees another nice-looking young girl, so long as she wasn't Jewish -- he had a deep hate for Jews and Italians. Tanga's mother told her saying, "Girl, I just can't understand how anybody could become so pretty in such short of a time as twelve years." She said she never stopped giggling about that.

The next morning Tanga Black was ready, knowing that under the circumstances she had no choice, being like all other slaves all over the world, (property) which was only one choice: do as told, or die. Some people believe that all of the slaves in the United States were colored (black) or came from some part of Africa. That is far from the truth; there were many white, and non-whites, a few yellow and other colors of skins of people because the traders knew only one color, and that was the color of money. They would sell any color of person into slavery; the only thing [that] looked good to them was money, not color of skin. It is said that slaves were obtained by slave traders from all over South America, and from around the world, but they all were not brought to the United States. Nevertheless, there were more black Africans in the whole United States before [the] Civil War or before eighteen-o-five, but after this country and England abolished slavery, then one country after another fell in line until all countries that were recognized had no more slavery.

Of course, as you may know, all nations on the continent of Africa are not black. I have worked with and for some older white men and met with some of their older parents who had not as yet been taught as children to hate people because of where, or [what] the color of their skin was when they were born, but had to admit that they were told some times that they were a little better than colored people, and depending on who you were talking to, the Jews were better than the Italians, but we were taught that nobody was better than any body else!

These old former slaves and a lot of people who were pushed around because of nationality- hate, of whom the KKK pushed the hardest, in some areas of this country, they suffered [more] than the colored people. These [had not] ever been actually in slavery, but caught hell nevertheless, and they wanted to reminisce about [the] bitter past, saying to the men working together in the old French market, all trying to bring a piece of bread home to the wife and them (wife, children, parent---sometimes, grand parent, and in-laws); the white and colored poor worked together for the same aim: Bread. The whites would say, "Hey don't feel [bad] because your folks were in bondage; we white people had problems too, and from what parents tell us around the fire place with tears in their eyes, It[alian] kids were beaten, sometimes to death; their girls were raped and sometimes murdered; they were burned to death sometimes in a house and whole families. The problem [stems] from the fact that the federal government made millionaires of some so-called immigrants who they brought in the country and were given -- contrary to the original Americans -- those immigrants were given large, large tracks of land such as hundreds of acres, without any control, law, or taxes, yet those poor bitter people among the first Americans, some said got here the best way they could, and some of them are still mad about how the US government allowed them to be treated so badly.

Our four parents said they came here from just about every country on earth, moving from places with pain, and suffering, fighting off insects, wild animals, Indians, and the British, plus death and hard work. They frequently had [to] move in and out of real jungles, fighting off huge spiders, all kind [of] snakes, and many different poison plants; the red ant was every where. They said their parents told them how they struggled real hard trying to tame this land, woods, and swamps to make it livable.

They would tell us that their grandparents used to sit around the fire and tell them the many horrible but true stories about [the] birth of our nation, the greatest nation of all, but we have faults. After all of that, then came the immigrants and were given everything: land, animals, tools of all sorts, material, seeds, wagons, money, and whatever else they needed and for as long as they needed it. They were completely subsidized, even with food, cloth, feed, medicine, furniture, cattle, plus a variety of domesticated fowls, and fencing material as long as they needed it. They got all sorts of farm equipment [so]that they were able to raise cotton, tobacco, rice, sugar cane, corn, pian(?) trees, all kinds of vegetables, and whatever kind of fruit trees that could survive in their area of the country.

But for the early, or first, Americans who came here on their own, like folks did, -- this man was the son of a very nice old man who I was working [for] in about nineteen-thirty. I was doing my work when the old man was there; he kept talking about things that were on his mind. Somehow, Mister Cambonio thought he could trust me, and of course he could! He had things on his mind; he had tell it to somebody, any body who would listen with some patience and compassion for the old Italian nice kind man, but if he kept holding all of bitterness inside of him, it was going to destroy him.

Mister Cambonio: "Sit down, son (that was my nick name); don't bother about your time is going on, son; I would like to talk to you if you don't mind?" I replied, "No sir, I don't mind at all." "Well, I know you colored people think we all hate you, don't you?" I said, "Why yes, I do. Sir, are you telling me that you love me?" He said, "Yes---as an individual." I said, "But not as a people? As me loving all of the colors?" He said, "Yes son; that's the way they raised y'all, but, son, most of us don't hate any body." [He said,] "Well, you see my great-grandfather brought my grandfather over here on a small boat that his family and friends built for the purpose of using to go the free world; the whole world was talking about the new world. My grandfather," he said, "told me many times the whole story about the whole trip; he said after their boat was ready for its voyage, they put all the dry food they could get on the little boat, and as much water as possible to set sail one day.

And they decided at midnight. We knew that we were taking an awful chance on those high seas, but we all kneed down together in prayer and placed our trip and ourselves in the hands of God." The old man was telling the story just like they told it to him, saying, "We had a few high winds but no storms for the whole twenty days at sea, and they [came] to this country with absolutely nothing, and my grandfather was a very young man on that little boat that had fifteen people on [it] coming into this country. We took a piece of land and cleaned it off. We," he said, "were four men, four women, and seven children -- three boys, and four girls." The old man Gambonio at that time was ninety-six years old. He said, "We were very poor, and lived on the, or off the, land, but we had a problem, and that is, we did not bring enough salt, and those immigrants had salt on two of their owned lands. They were very rich through all of that federal hand-out, and they looked down on us early Americans and refused to sell us any salt." He said they had some gold because from childhood, they used to pan for gold. "We had gold but no salt; we had to go away to New Orleans to buy salt with gold and we had to lie about where we found the gold. The rich slave owners had a lot of animals; if one would get lost in the swamps we would catch them and keep anything from a pig to a horse, animals they could never miss." The old man went on, "Son, we caught hell! They didn't know how much of anything they had, but if somebody don't capture them, those animals would have died or been killed. Our kids caught them and trained [them], worked [them], or ate [them]. They would buy our fruit, corn, and eggs, but [if we] tried to buy anything from them, they would almost spit in our face, and call our children wops or damn dirty dagoes----they hated us Italians too."

"Son," he asked me, "do you remember when one man was killed in that bank hold-up?" I replied, "Yes sir, I do."

"... when they hanged the six Italians?"

"Sir?"

He said, "Yes."

"... for one man?"

"They would even kick our children, or push them and call them names. If our young girls [were] caught away from [home] for some reason, you know just coming home? They may be raped and murdered and there wasn't any[thing] on this earth they could have done about it."

My father and grandfather were living when the Civil War was over, but this old man told me that at the end of the Civil War, he was sixty-six years old and, "Within three years, we all had moved to New Orleans, where they called us Dagoes," but he said they found out that New Orleans "...was the best, freest, kindest place to live for us Italian people in the whole south. However, they didn't seem to want us anywhere in these United States because the further they go north, the worse it got for us. Why? It was said that a few years ago there had been signs nailed on trees entering some kind of hunting ground that read like this: *No Jews, No Niggers, No dogs, and No damn Italians are allowed on this ground.*" The tears started rolling down his [face], saying, "Son-ny, I no dog! I dog, son?" I replied, "Hey, Mister Gambonio, let's just say *we* no dogs, huhh?" He said, "Yes, yes, that's right son." We both laughed about that; that made his son feel very good. He said in deep sadness, "Son, they hated us for nothing, we-do-no-body-no-wrong- but [they] shot us; they burned us alive in our houses; they hong us on trees; they killed our young men."

He [was] still crying while making such a statement saying, "Son, you know not one colored person, or their children ever called us nor [our] little children wops, scums, or dagoes."

That was getting next to me, so I began telling him about a few of our problems as a people who happen to be, no fault of [our] own, a dark-skinned human being. The old man stopped crying and said: "Mister Son," and I giggled a little at that. He smiled, saying, "Yes I know all about it, and wish I could help, but you know I can't."

I learned a very valuable lesson about bitterness that can be worn like garment. I have been bitter at times myself, yet I had nothing to offer that old man except that one thing that I had plenty of and that is love. This was a very nice old guy for a ninety-seven-year-old man who had to suffer because of where he was born; in this case, his place of birth was Italy.

Chapter 3

I had just heard the greatest earthly story of this age in my sixteen years of life. It sounded like one of the stories in the Bible that I could never forget because it taught my heart. In those days in the city, we had real cold weather down here, so we had the old-time fireplace, but we also had kerosene oil stoves for heat and cooking, but mostly fire wood, and hard coal, which we called "stone coal." It was so cold in most of those old buildings in the French [Quarter] of New Orleans. The rooms were very large, high, and wide, and full of holes and cracks in the floors and walls, so we had to sit in front of the fireplace, or close around whatever kind of stove we were using; the house could never get warm. The young just didn't run the street after dark. We would sit in front of the fireplace with our father, mother, grandparents, uncles, aunts, cousins, and friends -- all very old former slaves, some of them in their eighties and well in their nineties; a couple of them were more than an hundred, but we didn't know their ages.

Old man Ben Goodmen and morn Addai Goodmen would just sit there and tell us the hard facts about their thirty-five or forty years they lived in slavery and the many things that they had actually experienced from the belly to the grave. Having been in bondage themselves, they spoke with great emotional feelings.

Morn Goodmen told this and it moved us a whole lot. She said, "I was Master's daughter, his own flesh and blood and knew it, and he watched [me] grow up from a baby, and when [I] reached twelve going on thirteen years old, one evening [he] called for me, and told me saying, 'Little [girl], get yourself ready to spend tomorrow with me; do you understand?' I said, 'Yes sir, Master Ellefenta,' and I told mother, and we talked about it, and there was a young man slave about seventeen years old. He took me that night and we ran away just then."

Master Ellefenta had a wife about thirty-six years old. She said those owners, mostly the unchristian ones, treated their wives as if they were pets, and the slave women kept their mouths shut about their owner's business inside. They knew not to could be fatal. When those men marry those pretty young white little girls, all is well until they get up in age, like over thirty years old, plus the availability of all of those colored and a few others. Some of those girls were his own daughters, but that made little or no difference. Slave owners are somewhat like kings with sovereign power, and absolute rulership, and every body under or in the kingdom of any king are his subjects and must move at his every command. But kings are different from slave masters [who] actually own the people under them, which could give that little dog or other such animal instinct. Kings do not own their subjects, and have advisers helping them to rule, but not so with slavery.

If you check your world and ancient history in respect to slavery, which actually began when greed started making men go to war with neighbors to take what they have, and enslave the captives, for to sell, do their work, or for sex -- Even the God-Chosen people, the Israelites, the Patriarchs, bought slaves -- and slavery has been world-wide throughout history, and slavery is not judged by the numbers, because a lot of people are now, all over the world in slavery in different ways. In some unknown cases, there may be a few or more people, a boy, a girl, a woman, a man, young, old mental, or a single family member, and these things are still going on all around us right now.

The Israelite nation (Jews) went into bondage for four hundred years under the Egyptian nation, but they were not in individually-owned slave camps, nor were they under the rule of one person, but they were in bondage under the Egyptian governmental system of which they lived, unlike England and the United States, where the slave owners were allowed to practice dictatorship and for each slave-camp all over the south were able use sovereign power. [A man] could treat his people and wife, their wives disappearing -- only their say-so; no questions asked. If a person asked, "Where is your wife?" "She took off; she killed herself; her folks came to visit and she went back with them." That was all to it, just his word. A dictator has to answer to nobody; that's why if the master wanted a girl (a child), whosever's girl she may be, or at whatever age or race or color of skin, they all knew they were not free.

Aunt Goodmen said her sister refused to go to bed with [Master Ellefante's] brother, and she was choked to death, but it was mostly because saw him knock his wife down, and [she said,] "I don't know [what] happened to her when she fell, but she didn't move. I was here making up their bed. When he did that, he told me to get in that bed." She said she told him no, that she would [die] before I go to bed [with] any white man.

"He came to my kitchen with an ax and said, 'Are you coming with me? She said, "No, I would rather be buried beside [your] wife who you have just murdered," and when she said that and turned her back, he hit her in the back of her head with the butt end of the ax and she fell backward against him, and he was full of blood. She said she was about nine years old and cooking and doing the washing and ironing and general cleaning of the house yard and stables, plus bringing food to the second and third floor. "Once or twice a month, I had to run some white man," [she said;] "even the little girls had that problem. If a colored girl was raped by a white man, she was just raped. But if a colored man raped one of us we had to report it, but we would never say he was colored; we knew that some colored man [would pay] for it."

Old aunt-te made us sad, and then she made us laugh too, saying, "Look you little galls, um-mu show you something that you ought to know and you better learn; my body is not dead---and I can still move my hips as the Lord move the rivers of water." She stood up and tightened her dress around her waist, still small waist line; she started twisting those hips so at ninety-four years of age and had you seen her, you would have sworn that she had no bones in her. A little boy about ten years old exclaimed, "Wow!" She looked at him and said, "Why, you little earthworm, my grand- daughter just stopped putting diapers on you yesterday!" saying, "Son, why don't you wait a little while and if you do, you will be glad later on in life." His reply was, "Yes mam!" and they couldn't stop laughing with joy, respect, and love, for she was [a] darling of an old lady.

The strange thing about all of this was that most of those old people could read and write; a few of them said they had trouble reading handwriting but could do very well with all printed matter -- but all them had what they called their home-made books; they and they alone knew that these books existed, and they wrote everything they saw and heard, and everything that happened to them and others, like their relatives and friends. After the Civil War was over, they said they got together to make themselves some kind of records of their past that could be kept so as to read later to their offspring. This was out of their individual mental notebooks of memory, which was a life-time treasure to every one of them.

Well, one young man about sixteen years old who been in the Church from baby had heard so much about the late Pastor Johns; he had listened to his pastor who knew the old preacher personally and even served under him as a deacon in the Jons Town Baptist Church, and had become over the years deeply impressed with that country clergy whose subject was always the same: love. So one [day] we were just there listening to Aunt-te Goodmen telling us and reading out her home-made book the many wonder[ful] things about the grand old man Pastor Johns, as they called him, this young man stood up and almost crying said, "Aunt-te, I want to be a preacher, and feel the calling" and [said] that he wanted to be a minister just like Pastor Johns. They all said he [Pastor John] had only been down here twice, and the most we know about him, we learned right here around this fireplace. He was so nice when he was here until we stated calling him Pastor Johns and still do. And now we have learned how God in our times has intervened in our very being in allowing our old four parents to come over here, and took care of them and gave yo-all the strength to come through all of it and still have faith in God, and a whole heap of love in your hearts.

Now about the little girl and that young man who ran away to another slave-camp a few miles up the river, where he was known to be some sort of animal doctor---thus he was treated like a man rather than tool, because he was needed to take care [of] the many cattles they had. Ben had started working on animals from a little boy; he used to go in the woods and swamp and small animals that he would catch, he would train and domesticate them. They watched him as young as seven years old. The bigger he got, the larger animals he could work on: horses, cows, dogs or just about any that they would bring him; he was able to assist when a midwife was not available with childbirth. Sometimes in the case of white person's [being] very sick, it was either call Ben or else. Nanny, the girl who ran away rather than submit to her father and slave master's sex command, she and [Ben] became husband and wife, both of whom did come and steal her mother and brought her up there to live with them. This is the girl whose Aunt saw her master kill his wife and was herself killed with ax because she n____ to say no. Her and her run-away husband took their new owner's name which [was] Goodmen, which made his Pa—Ben Goodmen, and his wife Sanny Goodmen.

Many of the New Orleans slaves lived well into the twentieth century and told not all bad, but mixed, stories about their ordeals in their twenty-to-forty years of living under bondage, but as some of them put it, they only lived under the banner of slavery because, [as they told us,] "We lived as a part of their families and got along very well and peaceful with our owners, but a number of former slaves lived in the French Quarters of New Orleans, such as Moses, the Goodmen's, Henrea's, Smiths, Martins, Bornnets, [Boynnets?], Macklins, Willes, Jons, William, and a lot of others.

All of these last, or rather, most of family names, some of owners, were carried by many of the former slaves, but some of the owners would not permit it, but they were allowed to choose a last [name] for their individual families and so they did, of course. Those were former slaves or some of their offspring who would, when they could, just sit around and reminisce over their past life. Some of them could even remember how it was in Africa and where they came from, [but] didn't want to go back. At least not to stay, but most of them just wanted to tell their offspring how the Lord said, "If a [man] pleases God, he makes his enemies to be at peace with him," and how the Lord had made their enemies fight for their freedom. That was in nineteen-thirty; they told us that in many cases they were treated like free people, like human beings, as we know we are, whereas some slaves were treated even worse than any animal.

There was an old ninety-nine-years old man, [a] dearly beloved person who we knew only as Pop-Pop Moses. He said he was about thirty-four at the end of the war, "but my owner died seven years before the end of the Civil War; he left two boys, five and seven years old, and used to work at the Cabildo when there was going to be an auction in the Queen City, where men came to buy women (girls). What do you buy girls for, do you know? And the women came to buy boys, for what? Well, my wife brought those boys up from babies on her knees---they had lived so long that their owners was dead, and two boys that my wife took so good care of, I took them fishing and hunting, and sometimes for just a long walk through the woods showing them all kind of things in and about nature, before they were knee-high to a duck. I also made sure that they had a good understanding of Christianity and the freedom of universal love, and they both are now in New York City. One of them is a minister, but before their mother died, she gave my wife and I this little three-room shotgun house and a trust fund of ten dollars a month as long as either one of the two is living. And the other son was a medical doctor. However, the big house she gave to an order of Catholic sisters in New Orleans, but when they found out about the little three-room shot-gun house, the _____ wrote to the two sons in New York asking them to give that house to them too, but they were flatly turned down and badly criticized their satanic attitude and called them greedy."

Moses' wife was Sister Moses; she said, "I will never ever forget that day when I was bought off of that slave block. The people who bought me had already bought a young man and that couple that bought took me and that big fine good-looking man. [I was] scared of him; I was right at fourteen years old, and they took us outside of the Cabildo and stood us against one of those big old posts. She said to me, "Girl, could you fall in love with each other?" With my head down, I said, "Yes mam." She looked at him, saying, "How about you boy?" He looked [at] me, rolling them eyes, grinning and saying, "That's going to be the easiest thing I ever did in my life!" And we started grinning with each other right then and have never stopped. "Look at him!" He was grinning then! Then to everybody's surprise, she said, still looking at each other grinning, "and we ain't dead yet!" They laughed at that.

"When we went up there to the other place, we thought that we would be treated like animals, but to the contrary we were treated like what we really are, human beings, like most [of] the slaves that was living here, of all _____ so much so that some of us never felt like slaves. My first child was born when I was sixteen years old, a baby boy -- he ought to be about seventy-five years old [now]. We lived so much as a family until when ownership slavery was outlawed, the owners organized themselves together as a body in order to deal with people in the aspect of set laws that all of them was supposed to keep, because previously slave-owners were dictators. Their slave place was like a country that was under the rulership of kings, or dictatorship, but with much more power than either one of the two, because slave masters own the people, but kings and dictators just rule the people, not own them, as a slave owner does.

About twenty owners of them who picked Mister Goodmen as president, so "Mister," not "Master" any more, asked Ben -- not "command" any more -- but asked him if he would contact as many of the former slaves as he could to come to meet with them, and so they did meet one Sunday afternoon at the Saint Louis Cathedral Catholic Church in New Orleans, and old man Lund and [Lundand?] was to be the organization's speaker, for they knew now that these people were free, yet they had to eat! And if they [were] just let go without anything at all, they were going eat and feed their families or die trying, so they did meet, it was mostly to see how they were thinking. The speaker had the largest farm around, with more than eighty people on his place, most of whom he inherited from his father and grandfathers.

After he had told them who he was, and that now they were free, and are not owned any more by any person, and "the only master you have now is that God you bother" they laughed at that. [He was] saying, "and if any person wants to leave, all they have to do is to say so, and we by law must let go or else, and I don't like else! Some of us will give you money, the use of some farm land, an animal or two for you, a few hoes and fowls, (chickens). If we don't give them to you? Well? And let you go your way, your choice, but if you would rather stay on and work for us, for pay, so that you will have to work and be paid and buy what you want and need, and learn how to be independent, and no more hand-outs, other than your living quarters, of which we will add a room or so if you so desire it. And there are stores being built now, where you will be able to buy what you want and need with your money; that's what freedom is all about. Independence, the house and lot you may buy that it may become your own property (Independence).

"The store that they built was a plantation-type store where is everything you will need to survive; you will be paid every month. You will go to the store any time you want and buy anything in it, and if anybody working in that store forgets that you are free, I am going throw them out on their ears. I will build you a Church and school and some of you older people are well able to teach the children, and later on if you want larger Church, all you do is pick a piece of land, and I will give you the material that you may in your own time build your Church."

Just about all of the New Orleans slaves elected to stay with those religious former owners, but all of non-religious owners lost all of their people. Some of them were mean and hateful enough to kill some slaves by beating them to death. In some of the Christian families where they were only slaves by name, they said they had no real reason to leave the people who could have been nasty and very mean to them but instead they were so very nice and kind. Of course, a small number of them were so low down that to be called a mangy dog was much too good for them. Some of the people on those places were overworked and [under]fed. It was so bad that many of them ran away, and knew from exp[erience] that when a slave ran away from bondage, they would rather die than return and somebody would die with him, because the African would only kill a person unless he had to, so running from what he hated, and that was hate, which is the same as killing.

Popper Bernarda lived just below the city a few miles with a French owner, who [was] Master Winstent, but old Tryine—and his children and wife and them, (off spring) -- said that they had lived so well with those people until when the Civil War was over, they was so happy that we roasted a big hog, and all of us had a ball -- the former slaves and former owners -- and we were told then, "Men, now you are free to leave, all forty-one of you men and your families. Mister Winstent, not "Master" any more but "Mister" Winstent came over to my house. Bener [Benet?] Willis, his brother-in-law, had just died about ten days before, which [meant] he had to look after things.

"I had," old man William said, "what was known as a tree bench -- that is, a bench built around a tree. He called; then he called again, "O Ben!" I came out, and there he was, sitting on that old bench around that pecan tree looking so sad. I walked over and sat down beside him and said, "Hey, what's wrong with you?" He said, "Ben, now that you are a free man, tell me have [I] even a slave on this place?" All I could say was, "No sir." Then I said, "Do you want me to leave?" He yelled out---"Hell no Ben! You are the only friend we have, and if you leave us now in our sixties, we will soon die, me and Jonney, Anney, and my brother Downal. You and your wife are our little family. Ben if y'all leave us now, I know I won't live another year because I will have nobody to really talk to. We will have nobody to play cards with. Or to pitch horse shoes with. Or to go fishing, or hunting with, or who am I going to read the Bible with? Or who my brother and I are going to have a drink of wine with? Or who am I and my family going to laugh with like crazy when we want to be funny? You tell me, Ben. You know I only had two sons and one daughter, Ben? The boys, they went to New Orleans to live. I used to hear that they were having a time there, but now we don't hear anything from nor about them. Ben, we don't know what to think! But Ben, if y'all stay, we will give y'all all three of these houses that you and your children are living in, which will [include] more than two-hundred-by-two-hundred-feet of land, and we will be the same kind of family we have always been, because [if you] leave, I will worry myself to death and the rest of the family too. Ben, only six of us [are] left, and we are up in age; your wife Addimae, my wife and daughter, my brother, you and me, and we about the same age."

He said, "Hey Ben, will you play a game of horseshoe with me, Please?" Ben said, "Yes, and I'll bet you a pig that I'll beat you." He said, "Ben, you got a bet!" So we played, and he let me beat him; then he asked me to ask all of his former slaves if they would come here Sunday and bring the whole families, and my family will also be here, so they can be told about my family giving them the house and land that they live on and have paid for with their labor many times over, and that everybody will be paid by the [system of] for a day's work for a day's pay. We are going to roast two big hogs and plenty of everything for the grown-ups and the children to eat and drink -- everybody understood; all twelve families lived as a little village, with nine colored families and three white families. So said, they all lived and worked together before we were free.

"As other sorts of little settlements would spring [up], the people would [move] further apart. My wife and me stayed there five more years; then we came to New Orleans to live with my older son, who lived in the French Quarters of the city, on St. Peter street, and [in] about four years, he went to work one morning and that evening he came home walking, and told his wife he was feeling bad; he lay down on the sofa and within an hour he was dead. The _____ said they could not find anything to cause his death. We have another son somewhere in Chicago; we don't know where, but [we] buried Jimmy in the St. Louis cemetery in one of those high brick walls around the cemetery. You push them in the hole in that wall and [seal] it in with old bricks and cement." A few tears was rolling down his face, sniffing a little, almost crying, "...and our daughter, she and her family, came to New Orleans about three years before we did, with three children. Her husband said she got up one morning and told the children to tell me that she still loved me, kissing them, saying, 'I'll see you later,' and walked out, and have not been seen or heard from since." We were so sad, right at crying and some sniffing a little. There is no cemetery anywhere on earth like ours. Tombs in the wall?

Old man Ben William put a little humor in his true story, saying, "Yes children (you-all-ain't gon-ner-believe deis), but it's true: they put my Grandmorn in one of them old tombs in those grave- yard walls. One night I was acting a fool out there in the street, drinking and clowning as I passing one of those high brick walls, and I heard Grandmorn's voice saying, 'Boy!' so I stopped, and slowly turned toward the wall, andn't see (nobody) and I heard that voice again, which was Grand Moses Voice: 'BOY, you hear me?' I said, '(yes-sum).' 'BOY, YOU GET YOUR SELF HOME, AND I MEAN NOW! And if [you] are not home before twelve-o-clock, IT'S GOING TO BE ME, ME AND YOU! YOU HEAR ME BOY?' I said, 'Yes-sum,' and you should have seen me. I took off like a scared dog, and didn't stop until I got home and have not been out after twelve in forty years." We laughed and giggled over that joke for almost an hour. Of course, that was the idea; these stories are told by old people, some very old but very alive. These people tell pleasurable tales, sad tales, beautiful love tales, atheism, religion, hate, affection, satanism, suicide, bitterness, happiness, joy, marriage, rape, murder, lynching, incest, and burnings of whole families inside their homes of the filthiest, and most low-down and dirty, and worst kind [of] Sheriff Parish Politics of crooked, murdering, stealing, Adultery and rape in the history of the State of Louisiana.

Chapter 4

These old people said they weren't just telling tall tales, such as *who said, I say, they said, she said, he said, I heard morn or paw tell, master Jons said, the people said*, not any other so-said tales or hear-say tales either. I think, or I might be wrong, but -- and I believe this is true because I know them -- they wouldn't lie to me about such a thing, but not so with them. The stories they told were things that they actually saw, heard, and experienced. They lived in the North and the Southern Louisiana where all of these things went on for so many years, where so many young men ran away to go and fight with the North for freedom as human beings, which all people really wanted. The war was fought principally to unite the country, and secondary was to free the country from slavery, such as buying, selling, and owning people. And after the war, so it was, even though the Negro was freed from ownership slavery, but was still under political bondage for the next hundred years. The important thing about the Civil War was that, if the North would have lost, the whole country would have been under bondage, because if the Civil War would have been fought principally to free the slaves, [then] after the Civil war, the federal government would have subsidized the former slaves, like as they did with the immigrants.

In that beautiful Proclamation Emancipation, all Negroes, and some of the whites welcomed the words of President Lincoln, that all Negroes were free, but those were only words, and don't fool yourself -- words are wonderful, but in the case where the well-being of a whole people is in _____, words alone are not enough with all [their] power. There is yet something so much more powerful, and that thing is force. Words without force are like a body without Life; force is more powerful, has more speed, and it speaks louder and plainer, and coupled with action, it makes words come alive. "Free" is just a word, and without force and action, it will always be just an empty word (free) but the North had outlawed slavery ever since eighteen-o-five, and it backed with voting rights, which was full citizenship, but in the south the only thing the colored people got out of the Civil War was freedom from ownership slavery. Which was in itself a heavenly blessing through man and we were ever so grateful to almighty God, and President Abraham Lincoln, but the Negro got no constitutional protection in the South.

The fathers of our country, when they were making and placing this country's laws on the just and true and up-right order, we must admit, they did do a superb GODly job with those fine laws, but all for themselves -- how could those smart men forget some[thing] like murder and not put it in the laws? I thought every[one] knew that murder is and always has been every[where] on earth against the law, but the United States allowed lynching of Negro men, women, and children, and those old former slaves said they lynched, killed, and burned the people to death in their houses. This they said was Jews, Italians, Negroes, and dark-skinned people, and those men knew that all of that was murder, and they knew without any doubt that lynching is indeed murder, cold-blooded, premeditated, calculated murder and the law-makers in the White house in Washington just would not put it on the books, so that made all of the law-makers in Washington that fought the anti-lynch bill every time it came up -- they were as much murderers as those killers in our country, but mostly in the South. The Presidents and the congressional bodies of these United States sat back in Washington and put laws on the books in words only, but words without force were like a well without water. The Constitution says [that] everybody who is born in these United States becomes a full citizen at birth, and all citizens of these United States are supposed to be protected by or under its constitution and the word "exception" does not even appear in that rule; then why do we need a Civil Rights bill for the Negro people, who are among all colors, races, and nationalities who were born in this country? Also, then why none of them needed, aside from the constitution, some other kind of legislation in order to survive in their own country wherein they were born? Just like the colored people, why??

North and South Louisiana, even though just minutes apart, [were]yet as different as day and night. We have sat down a few times and listened to some real old people read from their home-made books which they had written many years before. Some were written only with the pen of hate and with the ink of pain, and [some] written on the pages of love, which were locked up in their minds like being stored in a steel vault; they tried to pass their African experience down from generation to generation -- they telling their children, and their telling their children and on and on, and [not] only to their kin, but [to] anyone, whoever was willing to listen. They were eager to tell their true stories to everybody they could before they died; and "…before those stories die within us," said old man Moses, saying, "Yes, that's the truth; those white owners can't tell you all those stories because just about all of them are dead. For some reason, they didn't live long, and if some of them did live to be seventy- five years old, in most cases, they were blind, lunatic, paralyzed, or [had] heart trouble, speaking disorders or some kind of nerve condition, or real bad, bad hearing, and these things were very common among slave owners; we don't know why, we just don't know.

"Y'all know Sister Maddy? She sings in the Church like singing is going out of style." "Yes, we know her very well; the whole city do." "Well, you think Sister Maddy was just a maid." One young man said, "Hey, you know I cut their grass, and I hear them call her 'mom-mo Mad; are you saying that she is actually their mother?" He said, "Yes son, she sure is!" The young man said, "Uncle Moses, how do you know that is true?" He say, "Son, Maddy is my sister." He said, "OH!" The young man said, "Uncle Moses, how about Mister St. Trena, who calls Sister Maddy 'Mother' -- is he their- their, their? Their brother?" The boy said, "Yes sir." Uncle Moses replied, "That right, son, his sister and brother, but you see, he came out like his mother, and you children would be surprised if you knew how many so-called 'White folks' are the grandchildren of some African women. The young man was despondent---when he asked, "But why do they have to pass?" the old man said, "Son, have you ever heard the word 'opportunity?'" The boy's reply was, "Say no more, sir." and every body exclaimed, "AMEN!"

The Burgundies bought that nice piece of property for him, gave x amount of money; we, the most of us went night after night and heard stories after stories. We would sit around a fireplace, especially on cold raining nights -- in those days it used to get cold down here in New Orleans; in those early times, there were not a lot of street lights in the city then, so the nice people tried to stay out of trouble by not running the streets at night. We would just hang around and eat nuts, mostly pecans, popcorn, baked sweet potatoes, hot buttered biscuits -- sometimes the potatoes were baked [in] the hot ashes in the fireplace -- with corn bread baked in hog cracklings and slightly sweet, and some good old shortening bread, also slightly sweet. Some of us would come mostly to eat whatever Grand Morn would fix for [us], and they do this with so much joy we would feel so gracefully welcomed in their homes because that's the way they treated us. We would go from one to another, sometimes next door, or down the street, or around the corner.

This night, we were in the house of Sister Anney Bunsh, whose grandmother was sold to the slave traders when she was five years old, because after her Grandmother's husband had been killed in a bush fight, [her grandmother] being such a beautiful young woman with a three-years-old baby girl refused to be one of the chief's wives, and she was placed in a stockade to be held to be sold, which was common in the whole world. [So] in 1823, her Grand Mother and little girl were brought to this country and disguised herself to appear sickly but was well able to work in the fields, so she was given as a husband a man who had two boys and a girl whose wife was dead; his name was Batest Bunsh, and my Grand Morn's name became Decrmimoshedo Bunsh, and my morn married one of her step-brothers who was Wonnia Bunsh, who was my paw, and in 1840, I was about seventeen-years-old when my step-paw's brother's son asked my mother and my master who both consented. He was twelve years older than me, and I loved my name - Anush. "I thought it was so pretty," [she said], just smiling all over herself. She [was] born in 1840, and died in 1946, which made her [a] hundred and six years old in the city of New Orleans. She was such a wonderful old lady and a loving person. She was said to be preoccupied with, as she put it, love is GOD: no love---no GOD, and the Power of Prayer cannot be measured, and whenever [she] was finishing a conversation with [a] person and assuming they believed in GOD, before leaving, she would always say to them, "Listen, such and such, don't forget to pray; He is waiting to hear from you."

However, in down-town New Orleans, when you hear people talking about Sister Anney Bunsh, it was always about how much she loved people, mostly children.

She said, "I understand that since the British outlawed slavery, that things are far different, all over Africa, where Christian missionaries long since have been sending people, teaching them religion, education, government, and English, and that is helping us to survive in this freedom as we now see it.

"When the war was over, we were asked to stay on. The three children came down and begged us not to leave, saying, 'Anney, Please y'all don't leave us; please, please!' hanging on my neck and arms, the little one crying. We brought all of the[m] up_____ and sat [at] the table, so we were asked to be seated; there was a chair for us at table. The little boy was beside my chair, saying, 'Ann, you not going to leaving me, hunn?' I said, 'No Chile.' My husband Caastall was looking along that long table as if in great wonder, saying, 'Whoever told you [we] were going one foot from here? We ain't going no-where. And is you going anywhere?' That was meant to be funny and it was. They laughed at that; they all were somewhat happy and laughing and eating, because we had voiced our approval to stay on with them -- of course, this time for pay. At least for then. Civia, the older girl [said], 'Oh, I am so glad that we are still altogether!'

"Then Caastall put some humor into their gathering, and turned their sadness into laughter. Now they were eating and drinking a very nice meal with some of Caastall's home-made wine, who was an expert in wine making. Then he told them a tall tale about one of the men who was a very funny man, tales that he had told to them, who said the reason he is here is because he ran away from Mississippi and he is the only person in this country who has only one name; if you say to him, 'Hey man, what's your name?' he would say 'Sam.' Then you say, 'Sam what?' All he say is 'Sam.' Then one of the men say, 'Hey man, you got de have another name, Sam!' He said, 'I have: it's Sam.' Sam said he and his mule used to pull logs out of the swamps, and you know that takes a big mule, hunn? And old man, Dann, said, 'How big is your mule, son?' Sam said, 'He's about forty hands high.' Dann's head was going from side to side in disgust, saying, 'Look boy, there ain't no such thing as a forty-hand which is twenty-feet-high mule nowhere in the whole world -- even an elephant not that high.' The men and women never stopped laughing at Sam; they called him 'Mister Sam Sam.' Then Sam said real sad-like, 'Boys, "you order been da" that morning when I went to get that great big old yellow mule; an old lady couldn't take any more Sam's mess, stood up saying, 'Wait a while, Mister Sam; just hold your horses, did you say a yellow Mule?' When she said, 'yellow mule,' she bent her head down and to the side, saying, 'Boy, in those African Jungles, I saw all kind of four leg animals, and I never seen one yellow one.' Every body was just laughing like mad; then he said, 'When I opened that stable door, that old mule looked back at me. I walked inside the stable [and] starting picking up stuff to hook him up. I bended over to move something, and he turned his head toward me saying, 'Sam!' I didn't even look up, and he said the second time, '**SAM!**' Not thinking that a mule ain't supposed to talk, I got mad and said real loud, 'What do you want mule?' And when I looked up frowning with surprise, he was still looking back at me. I said, 'Mule, is you talking?' His tail swinging all over me, he moving his lips, saying, '**SAM,** you go and tell your master that I am not working today, and if he does not believe you, tell him to come and hear it from the horse's mouth for himself,' and when I heard that I almost broke that door down getting out of there, and I took off running about fifty miles from here and didn't stop until I got right here." They started laughing at that for almost an hour and the little boy [said], "Uncle Bunsh, would you tell us more about Mister Sam Sam, please?" He said, "Son, Sam is just Sam; he [used to] move his head from side to side singing; he walked kind of [funny] to make the children laugh, and he could be as comical as he wanted to be, and he could act. He could out-run a small [child?] on his hands; he could eat and drink standing on his head; he could stand on a horse's back for a quarter of an hour; then, while the horse was still running, he could leap off the back of the [horse] to the ground on his feet. He could sing, dance, and tell jokes; people would just look at him and start laughing. In those early days, if one could sing, dance, tell jokes, and knew how to be funny on a stage, he had it made, but Sam said he had one aim in life and that was to preach the Gospel the rest of life."

Well, Sister Anney Bunsh said the last time she saw Sam was in the twenties when he had come to New Orleans to visit his three children who were all born here before he was called to St. Louis to pastor an old Baptist Church: "I have not seen Sam since, [she said], but one of his sons said he is still pastoring in St. Louis, Missouri, but he was not very well, but he told me that his paw, ever since he became a preacher, he has been Reverend Sam Sam.

Sister Anney Bunsh, as all of the Baptist Christian women, were called Sisters, or mothers; the men were known as brother, deacon, or reverend; she said, "Children if it's alright with you, I have another true story." Sister Marcle [Marcie?] Williams was her older daughter who lived on the other side of her mother's house. The younger one lived here, her and her husband and one of her three children, in the house that they bought not long after they came to the city. Of course, the Bunsh's still [had] a few dollars because, as she said, her husband was known as a hard worker and worked in the ward houses around the docks where there was a lot of food stuff available that was literally thrown away. Much of which was good food. A thing may [be] good, but after hold[ing] any food stuff so long, it must be replaced, yet much of it was fit for human con[sumption], so that gave them a lot of food, and they owned their house. So they were able to save a few dollars. Both of her girls had large families and good husbands, and most of all they had inherited a deep love for people, just people; of course that included young folks too. So the friends of her young Grandchildren did come, well next [to] all of them did come back, with about a half-dozen more people to hear a little about their African back ground.

The first thing she touched on was a statement about a past situation in our country that was also a world-wide scenario by the name of bondage or slavery wherein people buy, sell, or own other people. We are so racially mixed up, but we don't mind that of our past very much because those girls were under something worse and more powerful than a king or dictator, and that was under slavery being actually owned, a piece of property to be used at the owner's discretion. Kings and dictators only rule them, not own them, so the girls had no choice in the matter; we all are smart enough to understand property ownership. If a person owns something, he does as he pleases with it, whether it be a wagon, a cow, a dog, a tree, a slave, or whatever -- and a little boy, as [she was] saying [it, said,] "Sister Bunsh, are you tell us that you are not mad with white folks?" She exclaimed, "Mad? Mad? Hell no! To the contrary, I am glad that tribal chief sold my Grand mother and my mother with her three-year-old baby out of a stockade and brought [her] to this country. All of this was because that Chief could not have her body, and listen to this, young [uns], I am an American and not an African; they sold me like a bale of cotton into slavery. Boy, how would you [like] to be sold like a dog? I am free in this country; I used to in those jungles eat what was available, but in this land, people eat what they want, don't you? Don't tell me about Africa; my grandmother told us how those stupid chiefs, if a trader of slaves got his hands on a white girl anyway they could get her by kidnapping, captives, or any other [way] they [could] get [her], they would almost give their right arm for her, and that was just about all over Africa. However, it was said that a slave trader would sell his mother if she wasn't so old, but that was just hear-say.

"Now, let us listen to a most beautiful true story. This was in Jons Town. I don't know what they are doing there now, but after the Civil War was over, by then two of the three Jons brothers had died, and their children sold out to their uncle. Both of their fathers died with (TB)— which is tuberculosis -- so all three of the farms became a plantation temporarily, because the surviving brother Artee Jons was planning for his almost-nine-hundred-acres to ultimately become a town, which he wanted to be named Jons Town. There was a plantation, one on each side, of the Jons's. Those owners were old and sickly and decided to combine their two-hundred-acres of land, housing, and people to the Jons Town, which gave them thirteen-hundred-acres of land to their village or town which really became Jons Parish or St. Jons Parish, which had a young sheriff whose father's name was Sheriff Burgundy. He lived in that big house over there on [the] hill; he had one son and one daughter, and the girl [ran] away at the age of about fourteen, as she told the colored boy's parent the night they ran away with another mixed couple. She said she had to get out of that house before her paw and/or her brother forced themselves upon her: "They had begun to say and do funny things around me; I was scared to death," [she said]. And she was not shamed to tell some body – anybody -- about what happened in her house, how that her mother, the sheriff's wife, died one [day] and was buried the same day by him alone, which [was] rather common among them. If anyone asked about her, he would just say, "Oh, you didn't hear: she committed suicide after she found out that she had a bad disease and took some kind of poison and killed herself." Nobody believed a word of it, but no one could realistically question him because he was the sheriff. In those days he was the chief administrative officer of the parish, but the colored women after taking care of their house, children, and husbands, they enjoyed a little gossip among themselves, saying such things as, "Hey, child, have you heard?" "Heard what?" "You know, about the sheriff's poor wife. Poor little thing," saying real low to keep the little ones from hearing the wrong things, "Girl, you know he killed her, don't you?" Or, "You are a woman yourself, and you know that women don't just kill themselves that much. That's just too many suicides." Some other woman might say, "Well, child, you know how that is, when those white women who do not have Christian husbands, when they get between thirty-five and forty-five years old and a few wrinkles here and there, they used to get little thin line wrinkles on the sides of the mouth, and on the sides, over, and maybe under the eyes, which does not take anything from [them], nor change the womanhood, or her mental sensibility nor her sex capability, feelings, and warmth whatsoever -- you tell them that Sister Anney Bunsh told you this because she knows from experience that those women were killed out of pure ignorance; all they do is worry about getting old and dying. Those two things never bothered me, because, girls, if you live, you will die, and if you live, you are going either get old or die. Child, we see those pretty little white girls with those skinny little nice waist-line, and little or no butt to lay on, but the problem was that they wanted to keep their youth, beauty, smooth skin, and shape, and as we all know, that is impossible and their men seems to want the same thing -- stupid?"

Sister Anney Bunsh asked her daughter to please take the small children in another room for a few minutes. And so she did; then she asked we young men if we would be kind enough to leave just a few minutes too. So we left; she went on to telling them about when she was eleven years old, how her mother saw her trying to [move] her little hips around, "... so she called me inside one day and made me sit down and pointing her finger in my face, saying to me, 'Listen, little gall; I see you around here starting to move your little __x___ around like a woman, but when you get a man and if you want to keep him you better know how to switch, and move like those trees when the wind is blowing real hard, and in the meantime, if you have no joyful feeling like a dead log, you better pretend with damn good act! And give him all of you, and I mean every bit of? Do you understand little girl?' All I could say was, 'Yes Mam, Morn'." Then the others were called back in.

Now there was another darling old lady who had been brought by her great, great, great Grandchildren to spend a few days with Sister Anney Bunsh, her home-town friend, who she said lived on the slave place next to where her folks lived before the Civil War was over, "After which we, and both of our families, lived just next door to each other in Jons Town," [she said.] She admitted that she was older than Anney, but how much older she didn't know; she was over a hundred years old, but didn't know how many years, but she was in good shape. Her name was Sister Hanner Mae Dorna. Sister Anney said Hanner had a lot more experience than [she did.] Sister Hanner said, "I am going to tell some of the things that went on in those days." She didn't speak very good English because she spoke very good French, and of course that gave her an accent.

Sister Hanner Dorna began to tell the story about how they used to use their bodies as an art of survival for the Negro men and little colored children. "We colored women, or should I say, girls, you see, children," Sister Hanner Mae went on, "you see, we girls were nothing but children. It was not that we young Negro girls, [or] Spanish and Italian, wanted to go into our own house, nor that we wanted those old white men, but we had no choice whatsoever; we were under something like a king. A king calls most of the shots but a slave-owner calls all the shots. And I mean all! When we were sent for, we didn't do as several girls who refused to go and were later found raped and murdered, but we went and lived, so when I was sent for, my mother said, 'Well, now you have to go and if you don't, they will kill you, so I am going to take you to the door.' While we were walking on the road toward his house, my morn stopped and turning her head to one side, turned upward looking at me as if for the last time in great sadness saying, 'Do you remember what I told you a few months ago?' I replied, 'Yes Mam, mom-me,' and crying then she said, hugging me, 'Don't cry, baby; you know we love you and [God] loves you and he is letting all of this happen for his own purpose.' She [said], 'When the sun comes up, we see it rise, but will we see it go down? Will we?' I said, 'I don't know Mom-me.' She said, 'It is hard, but we want you back alive, little girl. I have been watching you walking around here, and if you can move that well on your feet, only God knows what you can do on your back.' I was scared to move another step. Then she said, 'Anney, I know you don't like and are scared of snakes; there will be some of them in that bed in your mind.' She slapped me on my butt and started back home; then she turned and yelled, 'Hey, you make that mangy dog think that there is a crocodile after you, and don't forget about those trees and every[thing] that mourns is not sick,' and I followed her words, and after days I came to visit my morn and paw, and they were so very glad to see me all in one piece. My paw said, 'My little girl, this is why I let you go because this way we still have you, and we are alive to receive you.' Then my mother and me walked out in the garden. She said, looking up at me from her knees in her garden saying, 'Look little girl, you know how your paw says that God is using people as his voice and that is all Christians, of which you are one, and don't you ever forget that you belong to God, is that right honey child?' I said, 'Yes mam; that true, mom-me.' She still kneed on the ground in her garden saying, 'You know the Lord gave us some nice bodies and our mothers taught us how to use them.' She was looking at me and said, 'You are a beauty!' ---- and that made me feel soooo good about my self! That was one day I will never forget.

"We were saddened to find out that just five days after my visit to my family, my master's [wife] supposedly to have run away and gone back to her parents in Mississippi, so when she wasn't seen around a few days, if anyone asked about her, he would say, 'Oh, she went back home to her folks.' It was said that white [women] living on most slave-camps had a hard way to go; in some cases, those women were so sad and disgusted that sometimes it would affect their minds that caused some of them to commit suicide, or the danger of becoming lunatic, or get too fat, or become rather low, sick or disabled, and all of their miscarriages were thought to be done on purpose." Sister Hanner Mae Dorna [said] these were things that white women worried most about, but the colored and the white Christian families did not bother about those things because they knew that if any of those things did occur in their lives, that the love and devotion of their husbands and family-members will take care of them. One of the larger girls asked her, saying, "Sister Hanner Mae, aren't all white women free now and always have been free in this country?" In reply, she took [a] deep breath---then said, "Well, honey, you see that's kind of hard to explain, because the only free people in this country are the white men and the colored woman, who were free to mix and do just about as they please even in public all over these United States and were even able to marry as far South as New Orleans, and this I know to be true, and living together was common down here in those early days where colored women were living with men, white and non-white nationalities, but the colored man and the white woman are not free and had to slip and plot, but people are going to get together; people are people. Because of the mid-wife working with the colored and white women, the mid -wives were mostly colored aged women." We asked, but she would not tell us what went on behind the scene if a white had a colored baby; she left that hanging: "Colored women with white baby was rather common then, and some is still going on and nobody gives a damn, what do you think?" The girl replied, "Here is what I think; it is satanic for a people in power to say, 'I can have yours but you cannot have mine'." A little boy said, "Sister Hanner Mae, I don't want any white girl, but I don't like not having the right to."

Sister Hanner Mae said, "That's Gospel truth, Son! Now let's go back to the stories in our past. Sheriff Burgunda was a hard, tough and straight-forward ruler of his parish, whose only son was his chief deputy, living in the house with his paw, who was the sheriff. So one day he was found dead in his bedroom when he was thirty-nine years old. When they searched the house, they found three large rattlesnakes in that room. How did those rattlesnakes get in that particular part of the house? That was the question. So his son moved right into the office as the sheriff of their parish. This all happened on the eve of the election for the Office of Parish Sheriff. After about a month, he began to harass the candidates. One of them said that somebody piled up a stack of dry weeds close to my house and set them on fire. The other candidate claimed that four of his prize horses were found dead, and they [made]sure not to hide how they killed them, so they both bowed out of the sheriff race, making young Burgunda automatically win the election to sheriff at the age thirty-nine years old, but the secrecy in respect to his father's death hung over his office like a waving flag, and the people were still talking about it, but not in public because he was so dirty and low-down. There was naturally still some gossip among a few folks here and there and sometimes under the mosquito bars which we had to protect us from mosquitoes plus bugs at night. One little girl said, "Sister Hanner Mae, do you mean that bugs would crawl up in y'all's bed too?" The old lady looked at [her] saying, "Baby, I didn't wan-um-in-nae because sometime I had more in that bed already than I could handle. If a bug bites you, move, whether you want to move or not!" They fell out of their chairs laughing, "… and some bugs bite everybody in that bed; then it's time for warfare. I tell you children, about three or four nights a weeks, I didn't want any[thing] in that bed giving me any more trouble." And a half hour later when they had stopped laughing, she told them that in those days, they had a very large influx of bugs, flying and crawling insects, and bugs, small and large animals, some disease bugs, snakes –"but by the grace of God, we survived and loved Jon's Town, which [had] been converted from Jon's Plantation to Jon's Town, and with the other plantations coming together which combined into so many acres until Jon's Town became St. Jon's Parish, whereas in all other states it's not parish but county." She said, and these are her words, that St. Jon's is becoming one of the greater Parishes in the state of Louisiana. "Someday, it may surpass New Orleans; we had a sheriff, deputies, jail, and a post office, which was in the Sheriff's Office; we had a small newspaper also, but our sheriff was power-hungry and willing to do anything to stay in office. To him, murder meant absolutely nothing, such [as] lynching, shooting, burnings, hangings, sex by force---fear of reprisal. All of this happened to Negroes, Jews, Italians, and all dark-skinned and Spanish-speaking people; killing of any one of those people to him and his bunch was like stepping on a bug! In that house where the people believe that he placed those snakes in his paw's bedroom that he might die from snake bites -- which was premeditated murder – [was] a very beautiful woman who was sixty or more years old and still looked like a girl who every[one] knew was his mother. She was said to have been a pretty little nut brown girl; we used to laugh at her, when we saw her in the yard out running the chicken she wanted to cook that day. The young sheriff knew she was his mother and how his father's wife was said to have committed suicide by his paw; of course he knew better."

Chapter 5

Well, now it was getting kind of late and Sister Bunsh, as most people called her who knew her, for she was such [a] fine Christian lady, said, "Well, Children, the time is getting late now, well past my bed time. Will y'all come back tomorrow night? And if you do I will have some popcorn balls and a few other things." They gave [her] a big hug saying, "We will be here tomorrow night if God be willing." She was still living in that same house that her former owner's children bought for her husband and her, which at one time she said she did buy. She was ninety-five years old when her friend and her were telling these stories, and she used to always tell us about her Saastall, who she calls "my Oh-man," saying, "my Oh-man was a very good husband and he knows how to make a woman feel good about her self." "My oh-man could find so many nice things to bring his woman; you know what he told me one day: I was about sixty-five years old then. He rolled over saying, slowly, being a little short of breath, 'My little baby girl, you are and look the same as when I first met you; you have not changed a bit,' and [I] fell in his arms," she said, "and that made me feel so wonderfully good." And when she finished reminiscing; then she went on to say, still smiling all over herself, saying, "Children, I am glad that the Lord is allowing me to live my last few years of my life in New Orleans and in this house that every body thought we bought but to the contrary, my former slave master's two sons bought it for us, my oh-man (husband) and me. I was like a sister to those boys and their two sisters; they told us when they were leaving for New York that [we] were like brother, sister, and parents "...who showed us the way to Christianity, and we are glad about that and always love you and want you to have this house, because we are going to the North to live. Now you be sure to pay your tax every year, and [here] is five hundred dollars in cash for you and Pop-Pop Saastall." Then he gave me a piece of paper saying, "This is how you may get in touch with me if necessary, and this is a nice house right here in the French quarter." They agreed that some of her stories were beautiful and brought a little joy to one's heart. Of course, it sometimes was a little bitter and brought sadness to our being -- such stories, as for [example], one like when she told us about her former master's children. She [said], "There were two girls that left New Orleans about five years before their brothers left; they both got married to men who talked like people from the North. We never heard a word from [them], none of us; then the two boys left and wrote four or five times a year and we would ans[wer] joyfully all of their letters. Then the letters [stopped], but we kept writing, and our letters kept coming. One was a preacher, and the other one was a medical doctor. We don't know what happened to either one of them; in the last ten years we have written at least twenty letters, and they have come back undelivered." She was crying, and the children were sniffing in deep sadness, until she whipped her face taking a deep breath saying, "Well, Children, as you know, we all have to face death today, or tomorrow, and whenever he comes, you are the right person, because, you see, death never makes mistakes." They exclaimed as if in one voice----"Amen!" (so be it).

By then, the young folks were willing and ready to listen to some of the truth about slavery, especially in our state (Louisiana), and of course in New Orleans, which is still the Queen City of the South because we have been told many things about past slavery times in our state, and throughout the United States by people who [have] never been there and don't really know what they are talking about. Then a young lady who was going to a high school that I know to be the only public high school for the colored people in New Orleans during the twenties -- the name of that school was McDonogh Thirty-five high school in New Orleans -- she said, "Sister Anney Mae, would you, -- do we talk like this --- you know (that's answering myself) -- right?" [Anney Mae answered]: "The girl said it – yes -- all white people aren't bad – No; no more for me, no." A little girl said, "Hey, how this sound? Um not goner live no life of hate, no—hear, see you later, hear, hate is a form of slavery – yes – you – hear – me!"

The old lady said, "Well, child, Pastor Johns taught us in school every Sunday [the]value of love, saying, 'If you love me and I hate you, we have a chance, but if I hate you and you hate me, we are in trouble.' The next Sunday he taught us about the very idea that they were still bitter about slavery, but the pastor asked us a few questions such as, 'Whose fault would [you] say slavery was?' So he waited for an answer, but none came forth. He went on, 'Slavery has been around ever since man began to war against his neighbor out of greed, but rather [than] keep killing all their captives, they found it more profitable to kill the old and disabled and sick, using the women as they wished, and working the men as slave labor. Now when the larger groups, tribes, nations, or whatever, had more slaves than they needed or wanted to be bothered with, they sold them to whomever would buy them.

'Now in the light of that historical slave background, let us put ourselves in the owners' place; suppose you were a poor farmer in some foreign country, and were under an unconscious form of slavery. Some of them were not able to do more [than] feed their families. If you were in their shoes and had the chance to be brought to a new land and completely subsidized, including some money, maybe to buy slaves, and you [were] given more land than your family could possibly work, what would you do? A little boy said, 'Pastor, you know what I do? I would just buy some slaves, that's all.' That's right, just say you could come to the new land, be given everything you need to make a new start in life; in that case, what would you do? They said, 'We come to the new land.' Now if you need laborers, and the only way you could get them was to buy them, what would you do? 'We would have bought people; we would have no choice.' So from then on, we understood, and have not been bitter any more, but love took over, which is so sweet."

Those old timers told us everything they could remember in the best way they could, but ever so often they would [want to] know why they treated them, Jews, and Italians so bad and [with] so much hate. "Children, they caught hell too, but after the Civil War, we tried so hard to forget that slave block, and started thinking about this wonderful religious and educational freedom and freedom from ownership, and thinking of how by the help of almighty GOD, we have lived so long on the type food we had to eat. And how we had to live, and how we under ownership conditions out-lived our owners, and most of their children, and how we took advantage of our new-found freedom by organizing our church, by going from house to house, until Mister Artee Jons gave us that piece of land, through the mother of Henry Goody Jons, who later [was] known as Pastor Johns, whose mother's name was Clementine Jons, the mother of Artee's three children, and other white folks gave us some money and material to help us and we [built] a church and called it the Jons Town Baptist Church, and it was still there when I left. Which was the first church for colored people in that area, and after we built our church, the churches started springing up everywhere, but they never stopped giving us the stuff we needed for the upkeep of the building. Then each village, one by one, built themselves churches.

Now, it wasn't that the white and non-white (mulatto) people didn't want us in their churches because they felt that they were better than other humans, which we were, or that they had another kind or type of God, but for one, it was the state law, and two, it was a matter of a class situation, such as, they had better houses, better jobs, better pay, and better educational opportunities, plus money, which has a class of its own. Of course, Jons Town was named after their former slave-owner's family name, Jons. Artee Jons the only one of the three original Jons brothers who consolidated their three two-hundred-fifty-acre farms into one large plantation, which ultimately became Jons Town. In the first few years of being free, the colored folk got along just fine living together, working together, worshipping together and gossiping together, until some of them began thinking that they were better than other colored people. These were people who were light-skinned, who the southern white man helped to promote discrimination among the colored people, and he did very well with his mulatto children until World War Two, when somehow they found out that they were just one of the Negroes of the United States Military service, because Uncle Sam already knew our race.

So the mulattos could pass for any other racial group, because there were other dark-skinned people in the United States military service, who were and still are classified as a member of the non-white black race by the whole world's white races who do not, and cannot [be] classified, nor can they accept such people as the Japanese, Chinese, Spanish, or Mexicans as white people, yet most of them are the finest, honest, trouble-free on earth today; some of all of those people were in the service, but only the American-born Negro was segregated and discriminated against, (why?).

I was born in these United States; there are perhaps fifty different nationalities in this so- called free country, with guaranteed protection of the Constitution of these United States wherever they live. If they were born here, they are citizens and never have need [of] any other bill, legislation, or anything like [that], or in the name of Civil Rights, which is already in the Constitution to protect any citizen and visitor. You are telling America in that unnecessary, unwanted, so-called Civil Rights, and a few years later, America, you pass another bill to give me a right that I did not have despite the fact I was supposed to, like every body else who was in this country, and that was the right to, of all things, to vote. Why only the Negro, who was born here, was not born with the right to vote, when everybody else who was born in this country was never denied any Constitutional rights?

I can remember when I was a young man, the only thing the laws of this country did for colored people was to free them from owner-ship slavery, but the colored citizen had little other rights -- did I say colored "citizen?" I was wrong. There is no such thing as a citizen-ship without voters rights, and you know, at that time the colored person was not allowed to vote anywhere in the South, nor did the North have any yearning for non-white voting. The only thing the colored people (Negro) was guaranteed in this (his) country under the law was prosecution of their self-made unwritten laws, instead of equal protection under the law. The thing about it is that very little of any of that has changed sufficiently since the end of the Civil War: one law for only the colored people; another law for white people; a third law for the non-white people, such as if a colored raped a white woman, he was sure to have some form of execution – legal? Or a white man raped a colored woman: if it ever went to court, it was thrown out. The same thing with murder; we cannot remember a white person ever having been executed for the murdering of a Negro anywhere in this country. If anybody disputes most of the things said in this book, let them just look over their left shoulder and tell me if I am wrong about this. The law of the United States says in as many words, if a person is born in this country, the very minute of their birth, they are automatically citizens of the United States with the full protection of the constitution anywhere you live, whatever your nationality may be, as long as you are not called "Negroes" instead of Americans, as they are as much Americans as anyone else born in this country. Now, am I right or wrong?

Now, some of these things I actually saw; a little of it was in the very house wherein I was reared; the white man tried to build a bridge between the colored people by putting light-skinned people against the darker-skinned, but [to] their surprise, that had been going on for many years. "You see," Sister Hanner Mae Dorna said, "there was a Baptist church in Jons Town, and of course there [was] a Catholic Church outside of our village among the well-to-do white folks. Well, some of the light-skinned mulattos -- not all mulattos were light in complexion, despite the fact that all mulattos are of mixed parents, yet many mulattos are as dark as their mothers -- but in Jons Town," she said, "a few of the light-skinned women started going to the Catholic Church, which [was] about a two-mile walk, every Sunday. They would get themselves ready, meeting and heading to that white neighborhood Catholic Church. They should have known they weren't wanted, even though their father could have been a member there. Not all real light-skinned colored have mixed parents; much of it could go back to as far as five or six generations, and when they would go there in a group of about six to eight of them, when they would walk in the door, they did like I used to do when I was a child. I used to go the St. Louis Cathedral Catholic Church, and as we would walk in the door, the very first bench inside the door was where they sat just against the wall. These were all women who would go for that half-hour walk. The men did not go; they had better sense than to [do] that and if those women would have continued going there, something was going to happen to them.

"One Sunday after Mass, they waited and went up to the priest to tell him what he already knew---how those white people and their children were mean to them. The priest finally turned to them and said in a nasty attitude, 'What you want?' One of them said, 'Father.' He turned his lips up at that. She went on, 'When we come to church, the members make their children spit on us and [call us] poor dogs, dirty, trash, half-white niggers.' The priest said to them, 'You know that you are not white people. I know you are not white people, and those mothers know you are not white people, and God knows you are not white people, and you know that these people don't want you here. But you keep coming anyway; if you don't like the way they treat you, that's just too bad, and I am sorry, but I cannot put all of these people out of this church for you. I respect you, but you are not welcome here in this church. I know you don't go to the Church in your village, not because they are not serving the same God that these people are serving, but the reason you don't go there [is] because you think you are better than those darker people in your village, and these people think they [are] better than you -- what's the difference? Hate is hate! So go to your village Church where you are welcome, where you are not going to be spit upon, and called bad names. That's what I would do if I was a Negro as you are.' One of them said, 'But Father, the reason we came here is because we don't want to be Baptized publicly in the river.' The priest looked at them a little silly, shaking his head from side to side saying, 'Ladies, I know, and you know, you are lying. Good day, Ladies.' He went in his office and slammed the door. One of them said, 'I don't know abut you, but I am going to be baptized just like my nut-brown mother,' so they gave up the idea that they were better, and they were Baptized into the Jons Town Baptist Church and never left; and she said two of them were living in this city now.

A ten-year old boy said to Anney Bunesh, saying, "Sister Bunesh, some day I want to be a preacher man just like Pastor Johns." "Well, young man, from all you have heard about God's true preachers throughout the

Bible, of which Pastor Johns was one, you see, Son, to want to be of all things, a minister (Preacher, Priest) is a dumb, but most noble desire for any man to have," she went on, sitting there stunned in an amazing joy at a ten-year old boy wanting to give up his free choice of life, such the willingness to go through whatever he must for the people he serves at whatever cost under God. He said he reads the book about Jons Town Pastor Johns, how he said he wanted to be as much like Jesus as humanly possible -- the boy said he wanted to do [this also]. She told him what kind of man Pastor Johns was, saying he had the ability to tolerate sweetness, bitterness, love, hate, good-will, bad-will, agreement, disagreement, madness, joy, beating, killings, burnings, lynchings and even to die in a Civil War. Henry Goody Jons, which was his whole name at birth, went to the North and fought for freedom. He said he would rather die fighting for freedom rather than live in satisfaction with bondage. And [he] stayed up [there], going to school and working on the [rail]road and there was in the village an older preacher, Samual Smith, who was pastoring the Jons Town Baptist Church. After about three years, the church membership began to fall off dramatically. He was just a country preacher and getting up in age; in front of the fireplace one raining, cold, high-wind night, [with] wind and rain coming in through the floor and walls, he told his wife and children while placing a log on the fire. After they telling him they didn't think that he had enough education or whatever else it would take to lead and serve a people who had never learned to love -- at least one another -- loving all people is even better -- Pastor Samual benn Smith who had been hearing his young preacher Goody Jons, who still had a brother, sister, mother and father in Jons Town, he said to his wife, Rose Bud, "I am thinking about sending for that boy Goody Jons." He admitted that he [had] let things get out of hand, and just didn't know how to bring the people together insomuch so they had begun to show hate for each other.

This was the strange thing about Jons Town -- that just about all of them came off the same slave place, and at [the] time, they were bickering between each other. They were even fussing about fighting in public among themselves, [so much so] that the sheriff had to be called in sometimes. He said, "It's bad, and it's getting worse." Pastor Smith just could not get the people to live like neighbors and understand that they are colored people and former slaves and because of that they are stuck together, whether they like it or not.

Pastor Samual Smith said, "Rose Bud, I have written this letter; I am sending for that boy --Old Henry Goody Jons -- to come back here and take over this dying Church. And this dying village." He said, "Rose Bud, I believe they [are] both are dying, and I don't know what to do about it." And his wife walked over to him, hugging and kissing him as she has been doing some twenty-some years saying, "That's right, my God Man; you just go straight ahead." He finished the letter and sent the letter by giving it to the two men who ran the rail car along the track, checking for any kind of defects in the tracks. They had to travel from one end of the tracks to the other year-round, and each time they would pass a gauge, they would inquire until they were near Lake Michigan and there he was working on the railroad. Well, when Pastor Smith gave the letter to the men to deliver for him, they needed a description of the man aside from his name. Pastor Smith said, "Well, he is a tall man about six feet, broad shoulders, not skinny, but not fat; he is a white-colored man, and a kind, nice, good-looking, loving person. After listening, one of the men said, "Hey Reverend, is he a preacher man?" Reverend Smith replied, "Why, Yes!" The man [said], "Oh, I know him; they call him white-te, but his name is Henry Goody Jons."

In six days, he got the message, and as soon as he received it, he gave each of them a five-dollar bill, which was more than a week's pay. While he was reading that letter, a couple of tears was rolling down his face. His nick-name on the job [was] White-te; all of the men and bosses came to him saying, "Hey, White-te, what's wrong?" He read the letter to them and after hearing it, they were so saddened that the boss paid him off and told him if he ever came back, he had a job; and they all said, "Good Luck, white-colored man," laughing it off. "We know you will make it, and we all love you !"

White-te, he got his stuff together, and wrapped his legs real well up to his hips and his arms up to his shoulders with garlic and dried red peppers to ward off and protect him against snakes and small animals; then he hit those woods. And six days later, the children were out playing, and they came running like wild and scared, hollering, "Hey, there is coming down the road a tall white man by himself coming to our village; come and see!" The people started coming out and calling for the Pastor. He said, "Children, that's old Goody Jons, your new Pastor, the son of our beloved Sister Clamertine Jons; let's go out to meet him. He is one of God's ministers of love." And as he was walking up [to] the people who came out to welcome him back home, he placed his right arm across his stomach and bowed himself toward the ground, saying, "Children, if God made you, I love you. And before you can hate anybody, you must first hate that God that is within you, because there is a little chunk of God in every one of you, and [He] loves you too."

In two [days], the news had reached the whole village, and they were stunned at what they were hearing about Sister Clamertine's son [who] had gone to school in Chicago, and now of all places, he has come back to his little backward village; that village never did get over that shock. It was said that when those two men delivered that letter to him, he said, "I THANK you for letting the Lord use you to deliver this message to me, because this is truly a message from heaven." Then he looked up, as if looking into heaven, and as if he was talking to somebody. "Almighty God, I thank you and please give [me] enough strength to get back home, and when I do, Lord, please be there to meet me, and never leave me there nor anywhere or anytime."

Henry Goody Jons went to fight in the Civil War with [the] Northern Army. He didn't have to really bother himself about the Civil War in respect to slavery, in that he had all of the traits of a French immigrant (a white man), so after the war, he stayed up north and went to school a little while. Then he went to work on the railroad, which he did not have to do, because his white father had offered to set him up by having him declared his legal son -- white: "I will register you a person and give you every thing I have, if you just accept being a white person -- please? And nobody will be able to buck you because of your wealth, and you will have power and be Mister Jons!" He was sixteen-years-old then. He was so full of anxiety that he fell on his father's neck, crying, saying, "No, No, No, my father, be it far from me; I don't want anything you have, but you, just you alone, is enough for me. You have done more for [me] than you will ever know!" He said he loved his father and his father claimed to love all three of his children -- his brother and sister -- their father gave them the land and money they needed to take care of some of the old and crippled people who had none to care for them.

They cared for a number of those poor people, with other people for miles around Jons Town. They knew how to live on the land; they raised just about every thing they ate. Their paw gave them hogs, cows, horses, mules, and plows, and three hundred-by-three-hundred-feet of land. Their African mother and French father gave them everything they asked them for and more. Goody Jons's first night back in the village, he stayed all night at the home his brother and sister had for the old and crippled people.

The next day, he went to visit Pastor Smith, and they were so glad to see each other again because he had been gone about_____years. They talked about many things, including the condition of the people and how much dislike [was] among them, mostly the women, and how it was spilling over on the children, so much so that the children were getting into fights, and the parents were taking sides, and he went on to say, "Boy, you know as well as I do that things are hard enough for us as it is, and without some love spread among this poorer-than-a-starving-dog- village, we will not be able to make it the next two or three years at all. He was so saddened for the church's sake. He continued walking the floor with cracks in it so large one could see the ground if there was not for the pet hogs running around that ate the snakes. [The snakes] would be crawling inside through those cracks; they had to stuff the cracks with rags, paper, and/or cotton to keep whatever [out].

Rev. Samual B. Smith said, "Jon, you see, somehow or another, I don't know, I lost touch with the people. They come to [church], but they don't greet, or shake hands with each other any more like Christians are supposed to do. They bicker with each other inside and outside of the church; they let their children fight with [no] recourse at all. Jon, some of them [who] live right next door to each other have become so fussy day after day until they [have] stopped speaking to their own next-door neighbor over some trifle. They even stopped borrowing a little salt, suger, cold ice, and other stuff. Jon, we all run out sometime. Boy, they even don't pass plates of food and stuffs over the fences any[more]." Tears rolling down his face, saying, "You know, Jon, giving each other over those fences such as pies, cakes, cooked wild things, part of a just-killed hog, and home-made nut candy and more, such as loving kindness, a greeting, a smile, or even that bow from person to person, from house to house -- All of that is gone, gone, just plan gone!"

Henry Goody Jons sat there dumbfounded; then he rose to his feet as a deeply troubled man looking up, as if into heaven, saying, "Oh Lord, am I big enough for this job? Lord Jesus,I am ready to try in your name; if you will, please let me show them your successful outcome of your marvelous plans for them. If you will only guide me every step of the way! And Lord, I thank [you] for saying 'Yes,' in my heart." Then Preacher Jon put his hand on the Pastor's shoulder and said, "Pastor Smith," in deep sadness, "don't give up on Jesus Christ; he has never failed. And never will!"

And that Sunday, Pastor Smith and Preacher Jon were on their way to the mid-day service, walking in the middle of the road, well-dressed, on their way to the Church. The little [girls], with their wonderful female built-in modesty, with their little heads downward but looking up, smiling, moving to the sides of the road while Preacher Jons [was] walking by, bowing to them, smiling, saying, "I love you -- all of you." After the little girls had shown their shameful respect, they came back to being little girls again, saying, "Hey, he is some good-looking, hunn; he is some kind, too!" "Child, I like that kind of preacher!" "Hey girl, he is some nice!" "He told the men, my brothers, 'I love you as if you are me!' bowing himself a bit to the women and saying to them, "Good morning, ladies; you look so pleasant," tipping his hat to them.

Well, when Preacher Jons arrived at the Church, the boys and girls were there awaiting the arrival of their new Pastor. He looked at the girls, stopping down in front of them, saying, "Tell me, how did you girls get [so] pretty in such a few years?" And "What did you do to yourselves?" One little girl said, "We didn't do anything; God made us like this!" He kissed the inside of his finger and gently touched her lips, saying, "You are right; God sure did a good job on you'al," and they are still grinning!

Then he went over to the boys and told them, "Boys, I have got a lot to discus with you young men. When you were born, the Bible says you were born a man-child. Now, you see those girls over there? Do you know why God made them?" "No Sir." "Well, those little girls were made for you, little boys, (young men), to be your wives, the mothers of your children, and to bring joy, and happiness, and many hours of real pleasure that God gave them just for you!" He tipped his [hat] to all the ladies, smiling, [and], without opening his mouth, went into the church. The village folks were amazingly impressed with all of this gentleness and kindness of this man. Many of those people had planned not to go to the Church at all because of the bickering, fussing and fighting, but the very next Sunday, after watching the peoples' reaction going and coming from church with that beautiful light of Christianity [which] was reflecting all over the Jons Town Village, and all that week, love was blowing through that little village like a mighty wind. And most of them came out that next Sunday, so much so that the young people were asked to give their seats to the adults. Some of the people said they were going to see what this good-looking handsome preacher is all about and what he is going to say about himself. They said, "We [know] how easy it is for [him] to be a white person; all he has do is just declare himself a white person. We know his mother, Sister Clamertine, and his brother and sister who are slightly darker then him and can in no ways pass off themselves as a white image of his French father, Mister Artee Jons. Pastor Smith said, "That's going to be our next pastor, if we want him."

So when the service was all over, they were all so glad that he had come back because his whole sermon was on love. He started by saying, "Righteous brothers and sisters, you cannot love, serve, and be Almighty's children unless you love neighbor first. And then love all people as if they are you. God's word says you can not love God whom you have not seen, and hate people you see every day. In other words, if I hate you, I hate GOD, and if hate GOD, then I love the devil. Jesus said you can't serve two masters; you must love the one and hate the other, or either hold on to the one and let the other [go]. I love God. I hate Satan because I love you like Jesus loves and loved the Church in that he gave his life for it." Then he walked down out of the pulpit and stood enthusiastically in front of the people, saying, "Children, this is one thing I am going tell you that I want all of you to put deep down in your hearts---which is your whole being -- and that is, you have to either love or hate, because there is nothing in between. Children, either you love every body, or you love nobody under GOD! And remember this, the word says [that] without love, it is impossible to please God. The thing that bothers me is that you spend so much time kicking, fussing, and squirming, as if you don't want to give up that old owner-ship bondage (slavery) which He has just brought [you] out of, until you don't have enough time left to say 'Thanks,' but this is your village, your town, your houses (homes). And you can make it a hell if that's what you want it to be, but if you will put, not just put, but bury in your mind, in your mind, that those little houses of two-and-three-rooms with plenty enough land to feed you and your family -- but in your mind those little houses and this small town should be to you every bit as good as any of those big fine homes over there on those hills (the hills were because of the occasional river flooding), but here you are far better off than poor people over there, with your hearts full of love for your children, for your God, and for all people including them, your former masters, because, they are old, rich, with a lot of land, big house, most of them are sick, most of their children are leaving. They are actually miserable, living in isolation, with greed and with their consciences, with all of the dirt and untruth they did to a lot of people such as murder, burnings and lynching, hate, rape, unnecessary mis-treatment of men women and children.

"As a Christian, to the world, you may seem to have nothing at all, whereas you actually have everything; Jesus alone is enough. Try him!" When he had finished his sermon, he bowed and said, "Thank you for listening. And I bless you!" And [he took] his seat. And the people stood and applauded. Then Pastor Samual Smith came to the pulpit and said,

"The doors of the Church is open for new member-ship; if there be any, will you come forth?" Eleven women, nine men, and fifteen children came up. Pastor Smith's whole family helped to write down the names; the address of course was Jons Town, La. He still standing, said, "All who are in good standing, please make it known by standing," and all of them stood to their feet. He nodding saying, "Thank you." After that was all over and done, both of them stood in the pulpit area with Pastor's right hand on Preacher Henry Goody Jons' shoulder, saying, "Now, Children you know this boy, don't you?" They all yelled, "Yes sir, we know him." "Well, I believe that the Almighty and most high God wants this gentleman preacher of the Gospel to take over this pulpit and pastor this Church, so now we are going to vote," walking down to the floor and said, "All of you who want Preacher Jons to be your new Pastor, Stand up and move to the right hand side of the Church -- that's all adults- to the right, and all of the children go to the right hand side of the Church, and all who do not want him, just keep your seats." Then after the voting was over and they saw that nobody kept their seats, they began to applaud, about two minutes clapping and making other noises of joy, all in thanking God --for what? They knew not, but one thing they did know, and that was that the holy spirit of [God] had visited them and filled them with joy, and when all of the noise of joy was over, Pastor Smith said, "Would you please dismiss us Pastor Jons?" This was the last time he [was] called by or known to use the name "Jon," because he immediately changed the spelling J-o-n-s to J-o-h-n-s, which was the name of their former owner who gave them the town, and of the town and the Church. So from then on, he was known as "Pastor Johns." Reverend Samual benn Smith, the former Pastor by his own choice remained a valuable member pastor [who] gave the benediction, like saying, "Will all of you please stand, and if you don't mind, will you take the hand of the person next to you?" looking directly at them and [saying], "Repeat after me: I love you under God. Amen, Amen!" And the people said they were simply amazed that a thing like this could ever happen in our little backward village.

In about three years after they had received their new pastor, a problem arose among them, so that they thought that for them and their village, that was doomsday. So that Sunday, the Church was packed but full of sadness, and his sermon was about the power of prayer and faith working together, but in the middle of his sermon, he stopped and asked the deacons if they would please tell him what's wrong with these people? One of them said what was bothering them was the news that everybody will have to start paying tax on their property beginning at the end of this year, and that was to them like a big hard puzzling thing to those poor white and colored people, so there was only one thing to do. So old man Rehoboam, a hundred-and-three-year-old man living on [the] edge of the woods -- cutters and sellers of firewood to the white people, mostly of the well-to-do, and his two sons worked with him by selling the fire wood by the wagon loads, -- he took a few young boys throughout [the] village, asking everybody to be sure to come out and let's talk about the taxes —next Sunday at noon. The next Sunday, there was not enough room in the Church to accommodate so large a crowd of people of different

--------page missing from manuscript------------------------

Then he went home and [placed] the problems before the most high God of Love and asked the Lord Jesus for a solution for those poor people.

Well, all of the people came, because they all had the same problems, yet they were rather at ease because there were no instigators among them. Then the Pastor came out to them and climbed upon a bench and stretched out his hand over them and said, "My good people, you all look like one person to me because where race is concerned, I am color blind; however, I went to our Father today for your problem -- I mean our problem -- and he has given a solution. The Lord God has put this solution in my mind for us. And according to [what] he has put in my mind, this is the best thing that could have happened to us. Now you go home, and tell the Lord you thank him for turning our sorrow into joy, and I would like for to trust the Lord and wait until Sunday at ten a.m., for there is not enough time now to go through all of those things in my mind. I think it is going to take about four hours or more to tell you the whole thing. When you come, please bring some food and drink, and bring more than you need. And bring everybody in your house, if at all possible, including all of the children and old folks; for sure, if you do not, the solution given to me won't work, and furthermore, God is the only one who can and will help you, for he loves you. And the more you love other people, the more you will love yourself. I love you and will see you Sunday, if God be willing. Don't forget; be there at ten a.m."

Well, Sunday morning at nine o-cock, the people started arriving with their baskets and jugs and picked themselves a spot of land spreading their quilts and/or blankets on the grass, and began to spread out their food and drink stuff for themselves and whoever, and they were all racially and colors of people were there, and by the time Pastor Johns arrived, they were all full of laughing and talking, eating and drinking and full of joy and amusement. The former reverend Samual B. Smith couldn't believe what he was seeing. Pastor Johns said, "One of you?... Let me see who?... Oh, brother Bud," who quickly stood up, "May I have a small cup of your home made-wine please?" He said, "Yes Sir, my Pastor." "I have been told that you make the best wine in these parts; is that true sir?" Bud replied, "Sir, I hope so." Not that he wanted to drink it, but he just wanted to stretch a point. Then he clapped his hands to get attention, saying, "Will you please come to order?" saying, "All right, you are not a dumb people." They all replied, "Amen!" He asked for Spanish families, who said their families were brought to this country by fraud, being told that they were coming to a free country that will give you everything you need to make a new start and get rich, but we wound up in bondage, which wasn't much worse than where we came from, but now it is far better here. When the people from Spain had finished telling their story, the people applauded, saying, "We know what you talking about." The Pastor asked him, "Are you going to be taxed too?" He replied, "Yes sir, Pastor Johns, but I don't know where I am going to get the money from to pay them, Sir." The Preacher said, "Brother Ponchoy, are you willing to do what I believe the Lord has put in my mind? If you are, then let the Lord and me see your hands." And all hands went up; then he told the people from Spain, and those from Mexico, to get out there in those swamp-woods and find every kind of pepper plant you can, and if you look hard enough you will find a w-h-o-l-e lot of herbs, bushes, and wild-seasoning plants out [there] that you can bring home and plant on your little piece of land, and give them names. Those white people will buy them. "And Listen," he said, "most of those plants will grow easily in captivity, and dry in God's hot sun, because there are plants, many of which you can produce, such sp[ecial] odors, flavors, and medicines -- all of you get out there and get them, and profit from them.

"The next thing I am going to say goes for all of you females: when you go to sell your produce, [be] very sure you go in neighborhoods where there are families living or where people congregate, for you know you have beautiful bodies, and you women know that you are good-looking, too. But do not make yourself any more desirable -- I know that is hard for a female to do -- to purposely make yourself unattractive to men, because if those men pay any attention to you all, those women will not buy anything from you, and not only that, these actions are also for your own safety.

"Now you colored people, you know those folks in town love blackberries, and they like to eat sugar cane, and they love pecans, and pecan candy, peanuts, walnuts, sweet potatoes, honey, green peppers, fresh and dried beans, leaf vegetables right out of the ground, fresh string beans, and don't forget that white potato. Now we will just have to get into the ground and work within it, because you know that most of that stuff is not going to grow up out nor under that ground or on most of trees all together by themselves. So that means we have to -- all of us -- get up off of our butts and go to work, and that's [all there is] to it. Now you colored folks know how to make some of the most beautiful quilts on God's green earth, and you have a lot of children who say they want to help their parents to help themselves. Hey, all of you who [want] to help, will you please stand and say 'Amen'." And the children of [all] the races stood and said "Amen" no less then ten times. "The thing about this is that you make them with the whole family, so start putting your family back to work making quilts, and one quilt a year will be enough to pay the tax on your house and land. Now you know and I know, that everybody can't mess around in those swamp-woods, but you can, and in those woods are worlds and worlds of nice large fat pecans, and a lot of other nuts out there waiting to be taken; aside from that, there are a lot [of] turtles. And a host of wild game and wild fruits. These are things that just about all people like; however, most of you know when those white men go out, many times they get stung by bees or some kind of spider, large ant, bug, or snake-bitten. Sometimes, it's just a matter of a high f[ever], and other times it's fatal. And when it is, they blame us, saying, 'That's the act of that Nigger God.' But you can go out there and get all of those nuts [and] bring them home. And have your children peel them, and when they find out that you have peeled nuts, snapping turtles, raccoons, wild rabbits, and wild edible flowers that you can get for them in a reasonable time if ordered by someone -- Or if you will, when you have such and such to sell, the white people will [buy] from you and will even come out here to [buy] as long as they think you are poor and dumb, but if you start showing them how smart and wealthy you are, they will surely stop buying anything from you at all. Now let me and all of you assembled here stand and say 'Amen' and 'Thank You, Lord'," and all of [them] stood to their feet and started to shout, "Amen—Amen, Amen. Thank You! Amen! Thank You," and didn't want to stop saying, "Amen, Amen; Thank You, Lord! Amen, Amen; Thank You, Lord!"

Then he said in joy, "Thank all of you. Now let us turn to these nice humble Chinese people. You may think that being brought so far from your country [was a] waste of time. Well, my brothers, that is not true any more, because we will not get any more pity, or handouts, nor free tax system here any more, which has made us lazy, and we have become slothful, and that is why we all wanted to cry when the state and Washington said 'tax,' but you brought some of the most wonderful skills and morals, and of course, honesty, to this country. Now, one of you tell me if these things are true. I hear that you make an art in growing fruit trees and that you master the drying fruit. If what I say is true, just give me nod, and they say you [make] the very best of hog lard, and that you make a funny kind of candy that we all love -- the children like to pull it; I like to eat it. And that you make a very good dry wine, and one of my deacons told the other deacons when I wasn't listening that one glass of wine will make your eyes tiger, tiger. They all had a good laugh at that. Sugar is good, and all of us love it. And it is as [free as] those birds up out there, and the name of it is honey, and those [woods] are full of it, waiting for you to come and get [it], and there is a whole lot of fish in those waters. God put them there for you, and wild game he put out there for you, and you won't take the time to go out there and catch them; those things are waiting [to] be caught, brought home, and smoked or dried. As of this day, there is no more being comfortable, satisfied, and no bother, and don't care, and just don't give a grin, and do nothing but just plain take it easy and even slipping out of here, going to buy wine, and I know all about it. I am not saying that drinking is wrong, but wine is actually good for you, but the amount you or I consume is what counts; the[y] speak mostly in terms of excess. If you don't know how to make your own home-made wine, just ask some one of us how. In our country, it is lawful for each family to make two-hundred gallons a year, but none of [it] can lawfully be sold.

"So you had a problem, and you cried unto the all-wise most high God, who gave you a solution to your troubled mind, and I mean a real fool-proof solution. At that, one I think is going to work too, and how do we make it work? By as of tomorrow, get up off of our butts and going to work and forget about the word 'tax' because some day there's going to be some sort tax on just about everything we use, buy, sell, or own, and I somehow believe that some of those taxes will be invisible tax structure. Nevertheless, somebody is going to have [to] pay for that war that freed many, many people from owner-ship slavery (some of us). It has to be paid for; then you tell me why one should not be willing to pay a small part of it." Then he said, "I want you to eat, drink, and be merry while I go inside the church to see if the most high God has anything else for you, and if he has, He will put it in my mind, and when, or if, I return, I will make [it] known to you," so in an hour or so, he began walking out of the Church door, looking rather tired but smiling, shouting, "Children, all He has put in my mind is that all is well with the Lord. We started at ten a.m. this morning, and now it is two-twenty p.m., and I am asking you for about thirty more minutes, but don't forget to keep your mouth shut, because if you don't, you will fail, for the rest is left up to you.

"Now there is one thing more in my mind for us, after which, we may all go home, and that is this. When you go into those white neighborhoods or in towns, be sure you do not make yourselves look good in your face, bodies, or in any ways attractive; when you wash your beautiful bodies, don't go around trying to show off as if trying to attract the attention of husbands and sons, because your aim is supposed to be to sell your produce, not looking for sex. Don't rub soap under your arms, so as to have some body odors; do not wear tight dresses showing the contour of your [body] in order to stimulate the lust of greedy men. When I was a little boy, I saw an old man robbing a beehive of its honey. "I said, 'Mister, do you want me to help you bring that bee-hive to your house?' He said, 'Oh, -- son, I don't want them bees; all I want is that honey, and after I get what I want, I don't care what happens to the bees.' (I guess you know what that means.) And wear rags on your head, and let your feet look unwashed, and don't smile with their men because you will be setting yourselves up to be ravished and/or murdered. You men know how the great majority of us men---not all of us want honey but not even one bee. Now you listen to me; you can't fool those well-to-do white women; when they see your action, they will quickly sense what you are trying to do and will respect you for it, for putting off [that]un-lady- like pride, of which I believe was given especially to women." Then he declared the meeting over by saying, "Today I have done absolutely [nothing] at all except act as the voice of the most high Almighty God, so you be sure to give [Him] all of [the] Glory, and all the Praises belong to Jesus the Lord." After that, he took a little food and drink from diverse family groups, going through them, greeting one family after another and praising God.

He mixed with all of the people for about an hour. Then he clapped his hands for attention saying, "Let us pray," bowing to his _____ and saying, "Almighty and All-wise, most high God, our Father, who is, and who was, and who is to come -- the Lord -- once again we come before you to say 'Thank You for food, drink, movement, hearing, seeing, and Lord, the only True God, the Creator of heaven and earth, and all that therein are, and Lord, we need you so very much. We need You, Lord, more than we need the breath we breathe or this life it self. I ask you to bless all mankind everywhere in the name of Jesus Christ, my Lord forever. Amen. Amen. And God bless all of you, men, women, and children. [The] first fa____ of your job has just begun as of this day; now that is all. And thanks for coming, all of you, Good Evening."

So the people began picking up their stuff and going to their homes in the greatest of joy and satisfaction, saying, "Now, there is a man who wants to be used by his God." One little girl said, "Morn, I like him; he is the kind of man who wants to do, not what he wants, but what God wants him to do."

Chapter 6

A Love Story Worth Telling

When Pastor Johns was about thirty years old, his father was his slave owner. Also who taught him the art of reading, writing, mathematics, and some law, for he was [a] lawyer; this was one of the three who were born to him by the African girl who he had bought off the slave block at the New Orleans Cabildo. Pastor Johns finally did get married to a twenty-two-year-old woman whose name was Saidy Mea, who was said to be a cute little thing. She was the woman whose husband had been found hanging from a tree with a note on him saying, "We saw that washed tomb that you built in your village." A___ had built a tomb to bury his mother in; he had no children, but she had brothers living in New Orleans.

Of course, no one knew how much money he [Pastor Johns] had made in the Army and working on the railroad in the North before he was called back home to Pastor the Jons Town Baptist Church. The people still don't have very much, but the little they have now is a whole lot more then they have ever had; their income was not more then three dollars a month. Some could bring in at times up to five dollars in a month, which was not bad considering their style wherein they lived because they had plows and a few mules, and they knew how to grow most of their food and had hogs, which furnished the bulk of their diet, plus the wild game and of course, a lot of fish. The hog could give them hog lard, smoked sausage, smoked meat, pickled meat, salt meat (salt belly), plus smoked and dried wild life. They raised their own corn out of which they made corn meal and grits and popcorn for the children, and enough corn for fowl and the hogs, and they had all of the eggs, and home-made ham, salt-back, and smoked bacon for themselves and for the old and sick among them. They did plant a lot of sweet potatoes because they knew how to bank them up in what they called a "tato bank." They would have to either build or find a little hill, then dig into it and turn it over and over again in order to sort of granulate it somewhat like a dust, then place a layer of potatoes and a layer of very dry straw, then cover [it] with a layer of granulated dirt. Do this over and over again until reaching the top, and they had sweet potatoes just like in a real bank, and they would draw out of that tato bank all the year until the time of the digging of the next crop of sweet potatoes. There was a vast number of vegetables. And fruit -- those people knew how to dry and cure -- of course, almost everybody had a smokehouse and they would use nothing more then pecan wood to do their smoking.

Now they see their pastor, by all indications a dedicated man of God, he would go into the woods and hunt for every game he thought was edible, bringing them home and preparing them with salt, pepper, and spices, and placing them in the smokehouse, or salting them down and drying them in the sun, and he made it that there was a lot of cured and dried food in his smokehouse, mostly for the poor and needy, and anyone else who asked. He bought a mule and made his own plow in order to raise a garden. Those old folks who were telling us those true stories in their past told us that after Pastor Johns came back home, having been sent for by the former Pastor, Reverend Samual B. Smith, there has been no lack of food for the old, living alone, the sick, the disabled, or someone who was just a lunatic, and no more barefoot children in Jons Town, and there was no more fussing and fighting among them. Sister Anney Bunnsh said that there has never been a murder, rape, break-in, or robbery in Jons Village since it became a village (town) in about a hundred years so far. This was, as he put it, teaching by example because, he said, "When you take on real love for people, you actually take on God, for God is Love." Most of the people tried hard to copy after some of the things that he said and did. When he was called, he went; he made it known that he was available whenever called or sent for, but not with[out] his wife. They went from village to village preaching about the power of love, telling them the story about the vast power of love and what love can do with secret fervent prayer, all mixed up together in faith and the ability to wait on the Lord. He preached so much about loving your neighbor until within a year, the people said that they could almost feel that Great Godly universal love that he lived and preached so much about in the atmosphere. When he mounted the pulpit, whatever his sermon was, his theme was always love. In whatever near-by village he went to deliver a message, he would not take any money. He said his aim was to spread the love of God in the hearts of people. "I have enough of everything else I need and more." Consequently, they gave him all sorts of very good stuff that he would take home to [the] sick and shut-in.

The white people would go several miles to Church. Because of the State Law, they could not join the colored people's church congregation, but they could visit, claiming to be writer[s] and sit in with pen and pad in their hand. Now there were poor people there, and even a few poorer people such as the sick, crippled, and the very old, plus the children of these poor and rather ill people, and a few diseased folks, all who needed some help sometimes, and "…when you help them, you are doing yourself a favor," he said. "Think: who is helping who?"

Well, two or three of the old people remembered the marriage of [Pastor Johns], and they all agreed that it was somewhat of a miracle the way it happened. "Well," they said, "a very nice well- liked, pretty young lady whose husband had been dead about six months, whose name was, or [was] known as Sister Saiddy Mae began sitting on the front seat, on the very front bench, for about two months, but on this particular Sunday, she was just sitting there, and after the service was over, just before the benediction, he said from the pulpit to the lady on the front seat: "Sister Saiddy Mae, will you please stand?" So she did stand. "Why are you seated on the front seat?" She said, "Pastor, I had a dream about two months ago; I remember [it] well. I was walking home in the road and a little _____ on a real big horse stopped in front of me: 'When you go to church, you be sure to take your seat on the front bench and wait.' I said to him, 'Wait, for what?' He said, 'You just sit there and wait, so I have been sitting here for two months, sir. That's my dream, sir. I am sitting here waiting, but for what I don't know." He was just standing [there], pressing his lips together with head moving up and down; she [was] still standing there. Then he walked down on the floor in front of her, saying, "Sister Saiddy-Mae, will you please be my wife?" She opened her mouth and fainted, and he caught her in his arms, and when they brought her through, she said, "What happened?" They said, "Pastor Johns just asked you to marry him." She said, "Where is he?" He replied, "I am right here." She [said], "Pastor, when?" He said, "Would right now be soon enough?" She answered, "No Sir." The church said, "Amen." Then he said, "Members, you know this lady better than I do. I have never been within three feet of her until this day. Now if anybody knows any reason why I and this woman should not become husband and wife, let [it] be known this day, and if not, then hold your peace hereafter. He was standing beside her; he asked Reverend, the former pastor to marry them off, and so did he, and she cried through the whole ceremony, after which he kissed his wife and said looking up, "Thank You for giving [her] to me, and Lord, make us worthy of each other until that day." Then he said, "Members, listen to me; this marriage was a spontaneous situation which I did not anticipate. Some of you may have in your mind that we have slipping around with each other, but that is not true. I am just as surprised as you are; this thing took me like a storm. I have never gone with this woman, or talked to her one-on-one, or [have] been within three feet of her that I can remember. I don't know how it happened, but I thank God it did." She helped him do all of these nice things that he did for so many people.

The wagon, _____, used to pass every two months or so, selling clothes, shoes, pots, pans, tools, and a host of different families' and farming needs, even seeds. Pastor Johns would buy most of the children's stuff, such as their little clothes, shoes, toys, and some big-city candy. His wife would pick out the things, and whatever it was, he would just pay for it, but she alone would distribute whatever [he] had to give. She told the people on the next Sunday that she thanked [God] for giving her someone to love and to really be loved by, "…which gave me the willingness to let my husband be the same person that he was when he gave us to each other and to his people, that he might try his [utmost] show them what love can do.

Some of the well-to-do white folks for miles around sent things for children and for men and women which were discardable articles to the wealthy, but to the very poor, useful, such as a few dresses for a poor girl or woman, or a pair of trousers for a little boy or a poor man or a few pair of shoes. Rather than just throw them away, they would send them to the pastor, because the maids, yard boys, handy men, and other laborers would spread the good news about the pastor's activities everywhere they went or worked, and how he served people of any color or race without pay. When sent—he went mostly to the sick -- there were times when sick white folks had sent for him and he went without a sign of race or color. Of course, these white people were Christians, and the Lord raised up all of the people whom he went to pray for, and he never went without his wife, and she was treated with the greatest of respect and she stuck close to her husband.

Some of the Spanish and Chinese, living on the outer age of the village, did come to Church sometimes with their problems. This Sunday, the Pastor asked the men and boys if they would meet with him after Church service, and so they did. His wife walked home with the rest of the ladies, but the little [girls] kept looking back, giggling and waving. One mother turned herself around and with a shout, said, "Little [girl], come on up here; you hear me? Those little old boys will be along in a little while." Little Sissay replied, "Oh Mom-me, I am not looking for those boys, morn." She said, "Yes, I know you are not; come on up here."

Just about all the men around came to the meeting. He said, "Gentlemen, I did not call you out here to try to fool you into some religious gimmick, so let us go right into the matter that brought us here. I want to talk to the boys first; now you young men from eight-to-fifteen-years-old, you [will] soon be the head of your household with your own wives, and your little children, and you will have to look out for the good of your family, the best for them and to them at any cost; even to the point of death if need be." Then he walked over to the men, saying, "This may sound like nothing more than just a hunch, but I don't believe it is. I believe it is a matter of ignorance on our part. Our children, us, and our wives are sick with loose bowels, and I nor my family has it. Here is what I think; I believe that your sickness is because of the water you are drinking out of your wells." One young man said, "Oh, Oh, that's what you called us here for?" He was mad while making that statement. The Pastor said, "Brother, I mean, Mister Deward, may I ask you a question?" He said, "Yes, you can ask me anything." He said, "Mister Deward, how many children do you have?" He replied, "Yes, I got four of them." "How many of them are sick?" He said, "All of them." The Pastor said, "Is your wife also sick?" He said, "Yes she is." The Pastor said, "Mister Deward, I would [be] happy if you didn't say another word until I [have] finished telling these men why I asked them to come here tonight, because I see that you are not interested." Deward said, "Now you just hold on now, Preacher." Preacher Johns walked over to his seat and said, "Listen Mister Deward, let me try to help this dying village----now if you disrupt this meeting one more time, you will be telling me that I am not a man and that [you] are going to throw me out of here." Then the Pastor said to the other men and boys, "I am now coming straight to the point. You have two things that's giving you your problems: you are cooking and drinking water out of your outhouse. Here is what I am talking about; if your outhouse [is] too close to your well, when it rains, your wells will gain water. They said, "Yes, the water be much higher." "But you add to the outhouse, and draw out of your well to wash, cook, drink water, for flowers, and animals, so if the outhouse is too close to your well, some of the waste matter from the out house will keep soaking [in] until it starts seeping into your much-needed water." A little boy stood and was allowed to speak, saying, "Pastor, you are right; we are drinking our own body waste, and even a dog won't do that, but what can we do, Pastor, move the outhouse, sir?" He replied, "But if we build a new outhouse, what will happen to the mess in the old one?" The boy answered, "It will just keep on oozing into our wells." Another boy raised his hand for attention and got the nod, saying, "I believe we ought to move our wells -- all of them – but, Sir, tell me what can we do in the meantime, Pastor?" He said, "Well, young [man], we have been in my house boiling our water, and that will kill most little bugs." Then all of them voiced their agreement to move their wells more [than] a hundred feet from their outhouses.

Then the Pastor asked the man who disrupted the meeting at the start if he had anything to say. He stood up and said, "Pastor Johns, and all of you men and you boys, I am ashamed of myself. I feel like such a mangy dog, and I am sorry, but I didn't know things were so bad, and Pastor I do not hate you. I am not that dumb! But may I make a suggestion?" The answer was, "Go Ahead." He said, "Gentlemen, we are all in the same boat and it is leaking badly; either we all work together to keep the boat from sinking, or we will all go down with it. Now, here is what I suggest---- instead of each family digging their own small well, let each two families dig one big very deep well together on our property line, in case the women start fussing. And the deeper the well, the better the water." The Pastor and all of the men and boys thought that was a very good idea and began to make provision to work together with the families next door to them, which Pastor John was hoping would become a common phenomenon in their village. They did get together and dug a lot of wells, much deeper, and in three-to-four weeks, they were all but cured and happy again.

The next Sunday, many more people came to church because they were curious about this man: is he a doctor, a scientist, or what? But in his sermon that Sunday, he unconsciously answered all of the questions locked up in their minds, saying, "Children, I know that some day I, just like you, must [leave] this earth; we don't know when. That is why I want you to be ready, because when that time comes, we will have no time to get ready. I have been trying to tell you, when you have a problem, whether it be a large or a small one, I keep telling [you] to take it to the Lord at once. I am the biggest child in this town and, like any other child, I am too dumb to resolve any of my own problems because I don't know anything; but my Father knows everything.

Well, he asked the children to pick a night to come to church, "… and if your parents come, they will have to sit in the extreme rear of the church and agree not to say a word," because a few days before, a little girl [had come] to him, crying, telling him that her little [brother] had been fighting her, so he asked, did she tell her parent? She said, "No, Sir," so his wife asked her, "Baby, why did[n't] you tell on him?" She started crying again. [Pastor] Johns hugged the little six-year-old girl saying, "Why are [you] crying now?" "Because if I tell on him, they are going to beat him and make him cry, and [I don't] want them to make him cry. He is my brother; I love him." Then she looked up at Pastor, saying, "Is loving my little brother wrong, Pastor?" He replied, "No, baby girl; love is never wrong." So that is why he called that meeting among the young folks. After the meeting was open, he said to the boys, "You are little men. You, according to the Bible, you were born a man-child, so boys, look over here at these girls and remember what the Bible said that God [said] when he made them. Will somebody tell us?" Their parents were all there sitting in the rear. The Pastor said, "Who will tell us?" So a nine-year-old stood and said, "How about me?" He was given a nod. He said, "Well, Pastor, you taught us how that God stooped down and made a man and put some breath in him and he became a real man. Then later on, I don't know how long, He made him—looking at little girl friend, grinning -- made him a girl and brought to him and [said], 'Adam, look what I made for you.' He was so glad that he named her 'woman,' but she let the devil fool her, and she did eat of the tree that God told them not to eat, but she brought the fruit and gave Adam a bite." All of the girls were giggling because they knew what he was going to say, and he said, "When he bit it, his eyes popped wide open, and he looked at Eve and said, '**Wow**!" His mother said, "You little ____," and it took five people to hold her. She was just seated there with the rest of the parents enjoying their children, but when he said, "Wow!" she leaped to her feet shouting, "BOY, YOU...!" Every body was laughing. Then the Pastor [said] to the boys, "Alright now, you know that these girls were for you to be the mothers of your children and your wives and the other half of you, but when God give you a wife, he is not giving you a child, a little girl to rear or bring up as you [would] treat a little ____: yell at them, push them around, hit them, even fight them, or demand a little too much of them. Your wife is not a tool; she is a part of you under God." He asked four girls to come up there and four boys to come up, and he had a bucket of watery sand, so he asked the boys to show their musculars, and so did they with pride, and he [asked] them if they could pick up that bucket of wet sand and place it on the bench, and so they did -- each one of them -- but the girls could not even move it. Then he said the girls, "Do you see why God did not give muscular to you girls?" "No sir." "Well, do you know why God made them strong and gave them those musculars?" One little girl came running there to the Pastor, saying, "I know; I know!" He said, "Tell us, baby." She said, "...

to take care of us girls and our little brothers, and our mom-me," and he said, "Thank you; that was most beautiful, baby; you are so right. Now I want a boy and a girl to answer this: were those boys given those musculars to beat up on little girls? Even their sisters and their girls? But first, there is a boy in here now who did beat up on his little sister. She is also here with the greatest love I have ever experienced in all of my life. She came to us, crying, saying, 'Pastor, my brother fights me but I love him; he is my brother, and she never did tell on him because she said if she did, they were going to beat him and [he would] cry and I don't want him crying; he is my brother. I love him.' By then, she was sitting over there crying, saying, "I don't want them to hurt my little brother," crying louder----"I love my brother," so he went over and picked her up saying, "Jinny, baby, I am sorry; I didn't want to hurt you. I love you too." By then, everybody was crying, even the Pastor and his wife. Then Jinny's mother, washing her face with tears, went and took her little girl out of his arms. His Paw got up and going to him with his tears falling to the floor like little rocks, and he reaching his hand to his son, who grasped it and fell into his paw's arms, crying, "Paw, I don't want to hurt her; she is my little sister and I love her enough to die for her, but Paw, I didn't know she loved me so much." His Paw replied, "Son, we all love you that much!" Then the Pastor asked the people if they would please stand. With his face drenched in tears, [he] dismissed them. Little Jinny was just under seven-years-old and [an] un-necessarily beautiful child. The next Sunday, Mother told the Pastor that she had something to tell the Church. He said, "Sister Morver, go ahead." She said, "Members, something good came out of all these tears this week; three boys came to my house telling me that Jinny is the kind of girl they would like to marry when they get big enough. Then one of our young deacons, about twelve years old now, asked me if he could wait for her. All I could say was, 'Young man, will you ask me again in a few more years?" And one lady said, "Sister Morver, I don't blame those boys, because if I am still around the next seven or eight years, I am going [to] sic my son on her."

When Church was about to let out, Pastor Johns asked all of the members, but mostly the children, to please come out Wednesday night: "… it is going to be a meeting for character-building." After the meeting was formally open, he said, "The meeting is for the aim of you to begin to improve your character, and how to build good characters in your children. The first thing to understand about life is that people need people, and that need itself necessitates respect for it. And the next thing is that people are as different as the weather, and that you are not the only person on this earth, and each other person on this earth with you is an individual with their (own) personal opinion, and you may try to convince someone and do everything you possibly could. And when you finish, you may find that that person is still of the same opinion. I might readily accept your opinion, but you cannot force your opinion upon any one. But the keys are these: universal love, respect, honesty, and the willingness to work. Now, get this. The more you love People, the more you will love Yourself; and the better you feel about individual people, the better you feel about Yourself; this includes your family -- All of them! Now, how do you feel about the folks at home? Now I am turnin' the rest of the meeting over to you young people, and here is an example: My mother was and still is the most beautiful [who] ever left the continent; of course she don't come very much now. She has a bad heart. What I am saying [is] all good things come from the Lord, such as how we look, how you feel, how you think, how you live, and how long you will live, and how you will die. And even our sight, our hearing, our heart, our physical, and mental well-being is all controlled by the Almighty most high God. Now, how do you feel or think about your folks, and them? Your father, mother, sisters, brothers, and anybody else you can think of; and if anyone would like to see a picture of my mother, just go home and look at your mothers and sisters, and you will see her." A little girl, eight-years-old said, "May [I] say something, Pastor?" He gave her the nod. She said, "My mother is not pretty but she cute, and all people that see me say, 'She is just like her mother.' Look at me." The people was laughing, and the boys were giggling, and another girl said, "My morn is beautiful, and my Paw is a good-looking, kind, hard worker, and my morn say he is a good provider." Another girl said, "Morn and Paw love their seven children more then any other people on earth. Now that is what all of [us] believe." A little boy said, "Our mother is so pretty that some[times] she have to run us out of the house because we just be looking at her." One boy said, "Pastor, if your mother was as pretty as my mother and sisters, she must have been some pretty!" A little fellow said, "Pastor, my mom-me, sisters, and my grandmorn is so pretty til it look like they made themselves!" Then got up one after another saying nice things about their parents and other parts of their families plus a few other worthy people, most of whom were sitting in the back of the church giggling and grinning in great pride, and the children continued and said, "Well, my mother is as beautiful as hard rain after waiting for it a long time," and another boy about ten: "Boy, that mother of mine, when she got ready for church this morning, she was looking so good to him that he looked like he wanted to ask her to get married all over again. My Grand Morn? When she get herself together and start walking down that road to church, you ought to see them old men looking, and I don't blame them!" A girl about twelve said, "Pastor, I told my mother that I heard my Paw tell you that when he leave work, he feels like he wants to run home; why does he feel that way? My mother looked at me with her head to the side and lips pushed together and said, 'What your paw and me say to each other is none of your business,' and she grabbed the broom and started hitting at me, hollering mad saying, 'Why you little pussy-cat, get out of my kitchen NOW!'" And a boy said, "Well, this is what happened to me: mother was stirring her pot making some rue for the gumbo; she was stirring that pot, and you know how that is!" ... In the meantime, the men were giggling. The boys was just grinning, because their mothers were there. "... so I said, 'Mom-me,' She said, 'What do you want, boy?' I said, 'Morn, what did you do to yourself?' She said, 'What do you mean?' I said, 'Morn, you are so fine and good-looking as if you made yourself!' She stopped stirring the pot and moved it to the side and placed the top on it, picking up some firewood and turned to me in madness saying, 'Fine and good looking!' started to hit me saying, 'Fine! Good-looking, Y You Little Tom Cat!' And I took off when she said, 'Tom.' By the [time she] said, 'Cat,' I was in the woods." This boy's paw and morn were sitting on the back seat with the rest of the parents, so he said, "Folks, it's a shame for any woman on earth to be so fine and beautiful as my mother! God must have loved her a lot to [give] her so much beauty to bring to this earth for my paw!" His paw had to hold his mother to keep her from getting to him. She said he went a little too far that time.

The pastor stood up and said, "Children I thank you for coming and for your participation. Now that you know how to think nice things about other people the same as you think of yourself, and to be big enough to let them hear you say it, I think this meeting has done some good in the character-building of these young folks. I am going to ask all of you to do me a favor. I want you to, not less then twice or three times a year, to ask your parent, 'Mother, do you love me?' The same thing with your paw, brother and sister, and never forget, to say, 'I love you too!' Now the reason for that is that wherever you may go on this earth, you will always know that somebody loves you because they told you they did. I would like to ask you two more questions before we go to our houses: one, did anybody in your life ever tell you they love you? If so stand," but NO ONE stood.

Then he said to them, "Now, tell this: In all of your life, have you ever told anybody you love them? If you have, please stand." One boy started to stand, but the Pastor was saying at the same time to [the] children, "I am not talking about your girl or your boy[friend]," and when he heard that, he said, "Oh," and set back down. His [mother] said, "BOY!" [Pastor] stood in the pulpit: "Here is how we are going to dismiss tonight; let us stand." He said, "Children, are you ready?" They yelled, "Yes Sir!" He said, "How do you spell GOD?" They exclaimed. "L-0-V-E!" "Well, how do you spell Love?" "G-O-D!" "Good night."

So everybody went home filled with joy and satisfaction, saying, "Now there a [man] that GOD is really using!" Some of them said, "We art to be glad to know what our children think of us. Of course, some of them went a little too far I think." They said, "The man is doing all that he possibly can to show those young what love can do. He told them there are some people who think that money is enough, but that is far from the truth, because money tends to make people forget the need for love and hope." They said, "Pastor Johns has given everything that he ever had in him to those children in this area and we would like that he never leave us, but like all other people on earth, the moment we come into this [world], we immediately head to our destination and never stop for a moment until we reach it (the Grave). Then Pastor Johns went on to say, "Further, Children, I am no exception." That was on the third Sunday of June in nineteen-ten.

After the church service was over, and the secretary had read the church report, the pastor beckoned for brother Benney Smith, one of his young preachers with whom he stood in the pulpit, and said in a bit of sadness, "Children, you knew reverend Samual B. Smith and his wife who has long since checked out (died), whose grandson's hand I [am] holding. I told [you] three years ago that if [you] continually let God use you as you have in the past, that some day you will have to take up where I stop and finish leading these Christ-like, godly creatures, full of love (Christians) all the way to heaven. The Pastor asked, "How do you know that Christ dwells in You? And has called you to this work?" "Well, Sir," he replied, "being under the teaching for so long a time of a God-sent man, who taught me more by examples of what love can do, and how to love the Church enough to carry them inside of you, and if you feel the calling of God to preach the Gospel of Jesus Christ, you must first be sure you have learned how to love people, all people, as if they were you before you preached your first sermon." Then the Pastor placed his right hand on the young man's shoulder and presented him to the people to be voted into office. The members seemed to like what the young preacher had said. Some of them said, "He sounded a lot like the Pastor." The voting was to be next Sunday, so the people went home in extreme sorrowfulness because he had served them inside and outside of the Church for more than fifty-five years with the greatest of love and kindness. He was like a brother, a son, a father, or a friend, depending on the circumstances. The next Sunday their young potentially-new pastor preached, and in another couple of weeks they will have the opportunity to vote for or against Reverend Smith. He and his wife after fifty years, they still walked close together, and if there were a puddle of [water], he picked her up and walked through it with her in his arms.

So on the forth Sunday, the young Reverend Smith was unanimously elected and became as of then "Pastor Smith." Pastor Johns had been working around the house, yard, well, outhouse, smokehouse, chicken house, beehive, tato bank, plus all of the grass and weeds and fence-working, as if he was going on a long trip. That Wednesday evening, he brought in a lot of firewood while his [wife], Sister Saiddy Mae, was moving about inside getting food together for them, but he had to finish his outside chores before dark because of a few snakes moving in the dark, so he did go inside and take a seat with his Bible in his hand, God in mind, eyes on the moving of his wife in the kitchen, and she said she loved it. On Wednesday night, they would eat their supper a few hours before taking their mid-week bath just before bed. He had already brought in the water, and the half-part of a wooden barrel tub. They had for supper---fried catfish, potato salad, pan-cooked dry rice, St. ----- beans; they sat there talking about the holy Bible over their meal, and a good while after, when it was about for them to go to bed, they fixed water and he took his bath, then asked his wife for another piece of fried fish -- the back bone part (middle). He said to her, "Baby Girl," (for more than fifty years, he had called her nothing else). He told her, "When I get into God's heaven, I am going to ask them if they need a good cook up there. And if they do, I am going to recommend you." She went over to him and kissed him with one arm around his shoulder, saying to him, "When they send for me, I will be ready!" He took his bath and put on his bed clothes (gown); then he showed her the four insurance policies that he paid five cents a week for each of them—which had death value of one hundred dollars each. One of them goes to his sister. So he went to bed saying, "If one night I go to bed and don't wake up, it's well with my soul," so they were just lying there talking about their wonderful past togetherness and about how God put them together. He said, "Baby girl, I have never stopped thanking God for giving you to me." She said, "I have been doing the same thing too." Then he kissed her and said, "Good-bye; I mean, Good Night." He went to sleep, and he died in his sleep some[time] during the night.

She, crying, called to her next-door neighbors on either side of her, in back, and across the road from her. She did this about five-o-clock in the morning, and within five minutes, the new pastor and five deacons, along with several of the older women and children, were without numbers, and tears were falling like a light rain, and at [?] o'clock, the sheriff's office received an urgent message from the state capitol ordering them in the form of a re[quest?] to do all they could to hold that preacher's body: An undertaker has been contacted in New [Orleans] who are on their way to pick up the body of Pastor Johns and prepare it for burying and return it Saturday afternoon and bury him Sunday. We have received more than [?] wireless messages requiring [requesting] us to do them this favor. They said they have been hearing so many wonderful tales and seemingly impossible deeds. If he was a fraud, we would like to know one way or another; we are coming looking for the worst, but hoping to find the best. The Jons Town News Paper wired phone calls from New Orleans to Chicago and all in between, many of which found their [way] to Jons Village by rail, by horse and buggy, and whatever. Since the highway was five miles from the village, a backwoods town, the newspaper could receive a letter in a matter of hours and did get six letters by Pony express, which may have cost as much as ten dollars to send. The Governor of Louisiana sent his message to this local sheriff, saying, "These are our Northern Visitors who must be treated with the greatest of hospitality." Both the white and the colored ministers wanted the church to hold the preacher's body until Sunday, who died in his sleep Wednesday. That meant that his body had to [be] sent to New Orleans to be embalmed and brought back for a Saturday night mourning Church service for him, which [was] known as giving their last respects! And for burial the next day. So they did.

The new Pastor during this ordeal was able to begin to show his providential leadership. Right away, he was able to bring the people together in the midst of a crisis. And negotiate with the City's funeral home to take care of the body of the Pastor and get it back to his wife and lay him out in the church on a cooling board, which was an ironing board lying on two chairs or so, and the body is laid on it fully dressed. Then when ready to bury them, they would place [it] into a pine box and nail the top thereon and bury them six feet deep; but in the meantime, he was able to get the people to do whatever it took to make their visitors comfortable. And he told them, "This means that some of you will have to give up your house, your beds, because, as you know, the State Laws Of separation of races." He went on, "I know we men are willing to lose two or three nights." The women started looking at one another, pushing their lips upward, eyes up, head slightly down. One old lady said, "Son, don't worry; you will be able to make up for that little loss in about a week." That gave the people what they really needed, and that was a good laugh, and when the laugher was over, they went back to negotiating, and they finally agreed to do everything their new Pastor asked them to do. When they were all ready to go, he stopped them saying loud and forceful, "Look, You Jons Town Angels, I want you to feed these people like they never been fed before!"

The next day, the new Pastor jumped in the pot --so to speak--- because he found out that the newspaper and most of the other folks that came there thought Pastor Johns was a fraud, but at least some of the workers at the Newspaper plant knew better; they had men and women working there -- some of them are reporters. About seven colored men and two colored women who kept the place clean, and do whatever else the office workers asked them to do, they were so very nice that the whole plant treated them with kindness. Those people came to see this thing that they had been reading and hearing about, so they came from far and near to prove this thing, to see whether it be of God or not, whether those things were the truth or a bunch of lies.

About nine a.m., when the death of old preacher hit the Newspaper Plant, it was good news to the boss and some of the other employers, so the boss called an urgent meeting. However, a few of them knew that those tales were true, but others did not, which made them argue somewhat. After listening a little while, the boss walked in and said, "The meeting is over. Let us go down there tomorrow and publicly expose that damn false white-nigger preacher, and let us take very good notes so as to write a whole book of everything we hear and see, plus adding own editorial comments." The next morning, while the reporters were on their way, a few miles away on that bad dirt road, they began smelling the marvelous f[ood] and spices of all that food-stuff the Jons Town people were preparing for their Church Guests who had come to help them mourn the death of their late pastor. They were so glad that all of those fine Christian people had come to their village that the white and colored towns-people placed themselves in agreement to cooperation as far as the state law separation of races would allow. The new pastor took time out to tell the people that state law did not allow the colored and whites to sleep under the same roof, except it be a white man and a colored woman---ha-ha-ha. That wasn't meant to be funny but it was. He stood there making this sad appeal to the Jons Town people -- white, colored men, women, and all children, to be sure to tell the truth and nothing but the truth to anybody who asked you anything about him: "Now, if there is anything he has hid in the ground, let's dig it up. If it's hid under a rock, let's turn it over. If it's bad or wrong, or any kind [of] fraud, I as much as any other person on earth. So now you tell the stories just like you remember them, and don't hold back --anything. Tell them about the many wonderful things that happened in this village in the last fifty years, by that Holy-Ghost-filled man who always said he wished he could tell, or rather show, the world what love can do.

The Church secretary was there to register any family and see to it that they have a clean bed to sleep in. Then she said, "There is well-enough room for all of your families, but we will according to the state law not stay in the house overnight with you, for fear of reprisal, but at day-break, we will come back together as equal parts of God's creation." They were in an area of three-hundred-by-three-hundred feet, with a few tables and benches all over the place. The village people and all of the visitors came out to the field real early and a lot of fried bacon and smoked ham, and eggs, and some slightly hot pork sausage, and hot biscuits, home-made butter, and boiled milk, and a lot of wild honey, and everybody were asked to please serve themselves. And those big city folks were eating like food was going out [of] style.

The first person to speak was a medical doctor who passes through that area about three or four times a year. He stood and said, "Folks, I am that doctor that's due here in two weeks, but when I heard about the death of my beloved Pastor Johns," with tears rolling down his [face], "I had to come help mourn for the man who taught me in what he preached, and how he lived. I knew the man; he wore love like a garment. His people of all these races you see here will tell you that love for man and God to him was like the hair on our bodies; it was a part of him." "Amen. Amen. Amen" was all over the place. "He taught me what love can do and the power [of] love -- it is the only thing that I know that can absolutely change any man and turn his life around completely. I know, and this is why I know: one Saturday afternoon I came in town. I knew my heart was bad from a child, but I am a doctor and I carry heart medication with me, but [this] time, it didn't work. My hands started turning blue, and I was slowly getting a little weak, and before I fell in the road, I stopped in the Church, and said, 'May I sit here and die?' He came over to me and said,

'Doctor Wattbirg, you are sick and need a doctor real bad now.' I said, 'Are you a doctor?' He replied, 'No, but I know someone who can help you if you will let him?' I said, 'Pastor, whoever you are talking [about], ask him [to] Please help me.' He laid his hand on me and prayed inward; then he said, 'Heavenly Father, please don't heal that old heart, but, Lord, please give him a new one, Please, and a new mind.' Then he said to me, 'Tell the Lord "Thank You.' I said, 'Thank You, Lord.' I said, 'Hey, my hands are not blue any more, and Pastor I am going, and those three little children -- I know what's wrong with them and I can help them, but wouldn't because they are colored, but I don't hate them anymore, and I don't hate anybody at all. Since that day, any number of times, I have given people up to die, and come back to see them still living, and [have them] tell me the Pastor prayed for them. I thank you," and he took his seat-----

Then a newspaperman's mother stood and began to speak, to the great surprise of her son and all of his co-workers. She said, "Well, folks, I loved the Pastor. He said one day at a fund-raising gathering, 'I love you whether you love me or not. You ask, 'How can he love and don't even know my name?' He went on, 'I love you because you are people, and I love people, all people. And I must love you as if you are me before I can love God.' That was the day I stopped hating people because of the way they were born. Pastor Johns is one preacher who has served his people well, but like all the rest of us, when on this earth our work is done and our time is up, that's it." The woman who was talking was the daughter of a German medical doctor, who was the grandson of a German immigrant. She went on to say, "He was much like another preacher I read about in the Bible whose name was Barnabus, who Paul said was A GOOD MAN, and [who] was referred to like this: *we are* sending *you our beloved Barnabus*, and I believe that there are still a few good men (preachers) around, of whom Pastor Johns was truly one of them. Yes, my paw was a doctor, and he taught me many things, and I have sat at the bedside of some sick, real sick, people with Doctor Wattbirg, who he knew would be dead when he passed again, but on his return, there they were telling him of some strange things to him that this man had done and said, that made them know that [he] had been driven by some higher power which we call Jesus." Then, in a crying emotional voice, saying, "You just can't, you just don't, expect a man any man to go so far out of his way to do so much for so many people, so many times, -- he and that pretty little woman that he said God dropped in his arms. It would seem like sometimes that he was nothing but [a] horn of some kind that God [blew] through," and she took her seat. Both of the people who spoke were Germans,---then the people began to change their attitude and opinion toward -- mostly the reporters -- toward the old, old preacher. A lady reporter said to a nine-year-old boy who was going around saying to anyone who would listen to him, "That's the kind of man I want God to make me be." She said to him, "Do you want to do all of the things that he did? You [know] he was a preacher man, don't you?" He replied, "Yes, Mam, and I am going to be just like that man of God." "Well, son, you know he did all of those things because he was a preacher man, hunn?" The boy answered seemingly in madness, "No Mam; No Mam; No Mam, Miss; that is not why he did he did those things!" With his head moving from side to side, he said, "Lady, you know why he did those things? He was just trying to show us what love can do." Tears were running down his face like rain because he was so hurt over the death of his friend and pastor. She walked close to him and took his little wet face in her hands, looking him, saying while looking down in his brown face, "Son, you have just captured my heart for Jesus. Now please, don't cry; you have just taught me something I wish I had known all of my life -- that beautiful thing called love!" There [were] other people there listening to them. She said, "I am just finding out what love can do; this is one thing it done for me already: love has given me more pleasant and peaceful feelings than I have ever had in my whole life. Son, will you do me a favor? If you will stop crying, I will tell you something you have never heard in your life." He said, "Yes Mam." [She] said, "Boy, I love you." He replied, "Well, you [know] we all love you, hunn? You know, I think we either don't know how or don't have sense enough to." The little boy said, "Miss Reporter, I am so happy now." She shouting, saying, "Hey, look at me; I am free. I have just been freed from the bondage of hate. Young man, I don't hate you anymore nor do I hate anymore at all, and I am glad about that. I never knew that freedom from hate could be so sweet. All of my [life], I have been wondering how those colored people could be so happy all the time and full of joy, calling on the Lord, singing or humming many hymns, mourns, prayers, and some chants all through the plant. I used to be bitter and troubled at them, because I didn't want them to be happy -- that is one of the ways that the devil-hate [uses] to enslave his victims. Pastor was known to have gone over-board in his anti-hate campaign. He told his people that hate was Satanic, and the practice of hate in any form is Satanism. You can easily see that they love us, their enemies. They were full of and had nothing but life and I didn't pity them. I was glad that they didn't have anything at the plant; we would act up in words or something, and we could see them saying, "Poor thing; help them, Lord." We have two, sometimes three 'colored girls,' as we call them, who are maids to keep the office clean and do whatever any white worker asks or tells them, -- and [they] say 'Mam'---and 'Sir' and 'Mister' to the whites, or they would lose their [job] and may be found somewhere; that's how nice we are down here, ha ha. But they didn't give a damn about any of [our] dirty ways. Wannder was just going along singing and saying ever so often, "Thank you, Lord Jesus," so I called her, and she came smiling and said, 'Yes, Miss Saiaster?' I asked her, 'Wannder, what are you smiling about, and what are you so thankful for?' She looked [at] me, moving her head from side to side saying, 'Poor thing.' I said, 'Well...' She replied, 'Miss Saiaster, you will be surprised!' (Then this reporter looked over to the maid and said, 'Wannder, you were right; I am surprised!') The other maid on the job was working just far enough to hear what I was saying. She looked up and said, 'Lord, I wish we could help these people and keep them out of hell.' She seemed to be so sorrow[ful] for us, in a deep breath saying, 'Lord, Please help them!' She looked also at that other maid and said, "Cheary Mae, thank you for asking the Lord to help us. Well, he has helped me. And I am glad about that because now I love you colored people, white people, red people, yellow people, tan people, brown people, and if there be any other colors of people -- which is God's business -- but I love them too."

Then another lady reporter, who was known as Ann, yelled, "Hey, hey, you fellow reporters, and all of you folks who have thought enough to come, let me tell you something about my past life, and as of now, this day, my life and my God. Folks; it's not that I found God, but was that he found me hiding behind that great satanic wall of hate, and I am glad he did in time. In my life, I was taught two things: (A) Negroes are not fully human and ought to be treated like any other low animal such as dogs, cats, and mules, and (B) poor white people was nothing but poor white trash, and all dark-skinned people are no good. Along with them, damn Jews and dagoes ought all to be put to death, because the earth would be better off without them. The colored people have little or nothing, yet seem to be so happy and always full of joy, and what I thought to be a funny kind of freedom, and [it] bothered me a lot, because I know they are not free, and yet, somehow or another, they are so very free. They know we hate [them], yet they love us; we would push them around, call them boys and girls, and even yell at them and call them 'Niggers' some times, yet they keep singing, praying, and still love us. They are the poorest people in this country, yet in some strange way, they are so very free. Even though I came up a poor millionaire, or should I say I was a miserable slave in my own rich troubled home which had nothing but hate wherein I was brought up, my paw became a millionaire the next year after I was born, and with all of that money, power, and pr[ide], all of which comes with money, my family were still not free in a lot of ways. He was a good father and husband, but he still lived in that bondage of hate which ruled over him like a hard task master, and he saw to it that his wife, son, and two daughters lived under the banner of hate and separatism. He did not teach us by the very words *per se*, but he made it stone clear that we ought to keep ourselves separated from all dark-skinned people, and [that] all people who are so-called 'white folks' that has not rose color in their complexion are nothing but filth and not as good as snakes. He would say, 'I like their money, but I hate the very sight of them, and I can't stand a Nixxx.' Sometimes, I wanted to ask him why, but just didn't question my paw. Not if you like living. One thing that he did take great pride in, and that was being the Master of his house. I came here to write a story, and in my mind, I had already started writing what I knew I would find; at least what I thought and was told I would find out about [this] dearly beloved Pastor Johns, and may the Lord have mercy upon his soul. I came looking for filth and found Jesus, and through him, I found out what love can do! And I am sorry that my paw is dead; because if he was still living, I would go back home and try my best to show him what love can do to the body, spirit, and soul of any person." Then Ann said, "Hey, y'all, should I say more?" The people shouted, "Yes, Please, Miss Ann, go on." She went on to say, "We were very rich, and had poor people working for us, not that he wanted those colored people around, but he said the reason he does was because they were damn fools enough to be trusted, and they don't even have enough [sense?] to steal money. He said the more you seem to hate them, the more they seem to love you; they are all a bunch of crazy people. This is the one thing I can't understand: those people are dumb enough to risk their own life to help someone who they know hates their guts, and we are said to treat our dogs and other animals better than the colored people whom they still think they own, and my paw wouldn't have it any other way. And he told us that we ought to know that we are far better they are, because we have a lot of money and everything we need and [they] have nothing, not even freedom, but he did not have every[thing] he needed. He was so sick in his stomach that he could [not] eat regular cooked food nor any fried food, nor any kind of seafood, and no sweets at all. He at forty had fallen off his horse and, aside from his eating problems, he had to walk with a limp until he was fifty-one, [when] he somehow got TB. And lived six months and died, but I found out those colored and the few others that lived near them had every thing they needed in Jesus Christ alone, and we had nothing but money, and I just found out that money alone is not enough." She said, "Folks," in a crying type of voice, "I can remember when I was a little girl around nine years old, my paw tried to poison a whole village of colored families for what reason I knew not, but he bought a lot of dried fish and pickled meat and had it poisoned in front of our eyes. Then as a false humane act, he had it brought to this colored village with a few whites such as Jews and Italians -- he hated them too. He may have been trying to get even with them because my brother six months earlier had raped and murdered a young colored girl, and there was nothing they could do about it, even though they knew who had done it, and my paw knew also and laughed about it, but they said the most high God is still on the throne. One day, my brother came home rather early for a change and went straight up to his room to lie down, saying he was feeling bad. In about ten minutes, he started screaming and hollering, so my mother and paw went up to see what was wrong with him, but he was hollering to the top of his voice saying, 'Get out of here; don't touch me! I am not going with you; you are wrong! I do not belong to you; you did not buy me; you can't buy me! I am a rich white man; what do you want with me? I don't owe you my soul or anything else. What are you laughing at? No, no, leave me alone; I am not going anywhere with you, and you can't make me go! Somebody help me, please, please help me, please come up here and bring me some water,' so I ran up there with a glass of water in my hand and when [I] walked in the door, he was on the floor and worms were crawling out of his mouth and through his skin. I dropped the water and ran downstairs, and told my parents, and they went up there, and came right back down. Then they heard some screaming outside and went to see why, to find their son on the ground, dead; he either jumped, fell, [was]pushed, or even thrown out through the glass window. She said her paw kept saying, 'That's them damn Nixx God doing this to me,' and the people did eat all of the fish and meat, and the sick who consumed some of it was up and about in a few days. Some of the older dogs, and all of the snakes and wild animals which slip out of the woods at night and eat whatever they could find lying around, a few of them were found dead, all over the place, but none of the people were even sick from the food and they loved it, and it killed all of the rats, roaches, and ants. The food killed every[thing] that ate it except the hogs. As for the people, they [were] glad for all of that free meat that they had been blessed [with] by such a person, but when my paw heard about what happened to all of animals and reptiles and how it helped the few sick folks who were actually healed after eating some of it, he knew they had eaten the food. Some of them had brought some of the meat to work in their lunch buckets. My paw watched them eat the poisoned meat, -- but he always took a couple of dogs with him wherever he went. As the men ate the meat, they threw the bones away, so when my paw looked low and beheld his two prized dogs were eating the bones and he tried to stop [them], but it was too late, he could not stop them anyway, and other dogs did slip in and grab a few bones and ran off with them. In two hours, all of those dogs were dead. He said, 'Angel, you can't even kill them damn Nixxx,' so I said, 'Paw, maybe God is on their side.' He knocked me against the wall with his hand in my throat saying, 'Why,... you little filthy dog, if you ever say that again, I'll kill you, you hear me?' But they were too late; I had already decided that some[day] I was to seek out that God who will fight for me like he was fighting for those poor defenseless people. I could not tell my parents, but I believed in GOD, the God of heaven, and I used to thank God for all of [the] things that used to happen to us, which I thought was God's way of getting even with us for all of hate and mistreatment. But now I am no more in the bondage of hate, and I am glad about that. As of this day I am free, and I thank all of you wonderful people for going through so much trouble to show me what love can do. And I thank God for taking that speck of dirt and mixing it up with love into a man and putting a little or chunk of [Him]self in him and sent him to us, and I will never stop thanking you for that, Lord." And the people applauded over and over again, and all of the reporters ran to her to embrace and kiss her, with the kiss of joy in the Lord, and the people were shouting to the top of their voices, "And God named him Henry Goody Jons, and sent him to this little dark, poor-as-a-spread-dog village. God sent him to us like a light in a dark room, and that's the God's truth!" They kept on saying, "Amen! Praise the Lord," over and over, and over again. She yelled, "Thank God for Pastor Johns!" They were trying to get her to hear their satisfaction with all she had said, and about her being saved in the arms of love. She was so glad that she could not stop smiling, saying, "Oh, I feel so good about myself now. I can say like the man would always [say], "I love because you are people, and I love people, all people, and I am glad about that!"

Then an old man named Immanuel Zerah stood up slowly, moving himself, walked over to a lady reporter. "I am an old man, well over a hundred years old; if yo'all will hear me, I have seen a few good preachers in my lifetime who would have rather been dead than to be willing to live the kind of life that this [man] lived, by giving all he could and receiving nothing by choice. Old Goody Jons said he enjoyed the blessing of giving because people have given very much for many reasons, but the only time giving really counts is when one gives oneself. And that's what he did; I am not implying that your preachers in your towns and villages are not faithful, meaningful, outstanding, loving, God-fearing, truthful, chosen men of Almighty God, nor am I saying that there are not still a lot of good men all over the world; some may even be better men then our pastor Johns, and that's for sure. However, he was not just an ordinary preacher-man; he had a way with the people that sometimes we could not understand. Then deep frowns filled his face, eyes half-closed, biting his bottom lip, and exclaimed, "A funny thing about this man: whenever something was wrong with us, or the children were sick, before you could shake a stick, there he was, and I don't know how, why, or what? But every time that preacher came, when he left, he had been of some kind of help; how can any human being (man) love everybody like that?" He went on, "You know what that man said when I asked him did he love those who hated him so very much? You know what his reply was? He never stopped doing what he was doing. I was stunned when he said, 'Brother Deacon, I love everybody God made.' That almost took my breath, then he stopped fixing those children's shoes and turned to me saying, 'Brother Deacon, are you talking about humans, **people?'** I said, 'Oh yes.' All he said was, 'Yes; I love all of um!' I just picked up my hat and walked off talking to myself, saying, 'Well, come, after living more then a hundred years with hate and he taught me how to love people, all people, in just ten minutes."

Then Miss Nancy, one of the lady newspaper reporters, saw a young girl seated all by herself and went over to her; she was just sitting there sorrowing. So Nancy reached out her hand to the girl saying, "Young lady, would you talk to me?" The girl reached out to the reporter. The girl was about fourteen years old, saying, "Miss, what did you call me?" The "nice lady," as the towns-people had named her, said, "What is your name?" The girl said, "My name is Carria." Nancy said, "Miss Carria, that is a very nice name. Oh yes, you asked what did I call you? I called you 'young lady,' is that alright?" "Oh yes, I am thankful, but as most people know, we are never called 'ladies,' 'Miss,' 'Mister,' 'women,' 'gentlemen,' nor anything like that. All we are called are 'boys,' 'girls,' 'old man' or 'old woman,' and you called me 'Miss Carria.' Thank You, Miss Nancy!" She said, "You are welcome, Miss Carria," who replied, "You are a nice lady, Miss Nancy," who answered, "You are also a nice lady, Miss Carria," and they were laughing so much until people had gathered and asked, "Nancy, what was so funny with you two?" And Miss [Nancy] said to them, "Listen to this: Hey, Miss Carria," She said, "Yes Miss Nancy?" "Oh yes, Miss Carria," "Miss Nancy, I have a story for you." "Oh, you do, Miss Carria?" "Yes, Miss Nancy." "Miss Carria, when do you want to tell me this story?" "Miss Carria, when [you] are ready." "Miss Nice Lady...," "You are a nice lady too, Miss Carria." The people were laughing like crazy, so the reporter said, "Miss Carria, did you know the preacher?" [She] said, "Oh yes, I sure did!" with her head going up and down. The rest of the reporters moved close in to listen for some mess from this girl's action, which was the reason why they came in the first place. One of the reporters, John, asked the girl in a sort [of] pitying voice like this, "Honey, did you love Pastor Johns?" With her head back little to the side, looking upward into who knows what, she said, "Oh yes; yes sir, I indeed deeply loved my Pastor. Yes, I loved him next to God." The reporters were waiting to hear some dirt, or anything bad, but she was so filled with emotion and looking back in her mind, she leaped to her feet saying, "Let me tell you the best thing he taught me," and every[one] started moving in closer to hear this story, for they could see that she was full of emotion. Some of them said "Hey, this sounds like some kind of child mischievousness."

"Well, somehow I did not like the Chinese people, and I don't know why, but Miss Nancy-- just think of me – me, of all people? A Negro who all [think of] as the scum of the earth, because of the way I was born, something I had nothing to do with at all, and there I was talking about I don't like some race or color, or a people, because of the way they were born, as if we had a choice or whose fault is it that we are whatever we are? The Pastor used to watch us children when we were leaving Church-school. That day, he saw me laughing at and being unkind to some Chinese children for no other reason than they were Chinese. The next day, when the sun was going down, I was in the backyard, playing with my little sisters [and] brother, when my mother called me, saying, 'Carria, Pastor Johns wants to talk to you; do you know why?' I said, 'No mam.' She said, 'Come on, Pastor; she is in there.' I was sitting there troubled within me, my little knees knocking together. When he came in, he did not [look] at me but pulled up a chair and sat in front of me and said, 'Darling, baby child, don't be afraid. I could[n't] love you any more if you were me.' Those words were so sweet, until it made me grin all over my little self. Then he said, 'Baby child, listen to me; don't you ever again try to make God mad with you. What I mean is -- never belittle anybody, or look down on a person or group, or any race of people. I don't care how bad they may look to you, or how worse off they may be than you are. You many think their eyes are funny, or you may not like their nose, or their lips, or their hair, or they may be too fat, or too thin, or you may not like the color of their skin, or the way they walk, or talk, or the way they are built. Baby child, would you say that's the way God made them?' With tears running down our faces as if being in a hard rain, and I was sniffing so loud that my mother came to check, and when she heard me saying, 'Yes sir, dear Pastor, I am sorry and I will never hate any one of God's children again,' she couldn't hold any longer; she cried out, 'Oh Lord, have mercy on my baby and my Pastor, Please.' He went on, 'and Honey, don't ever in your life discredit anybody for any reason, anytime, or anywhere for your own purpose, because you see, Little Tree, you can find a little bad in some of the very best of people. And you may find a little good in the worst of people, Now, there may just a little bit, but nevertheless it's there. Now you may be better than some people, but only in character, because you can never be better than people because you are people -- just one of all of the rest of us headed for the grave, and we will all meet there some day -- people no more, no less, just people.'

"Now [the] bigger Chinese girl's name was Town-ton. She was such a beautiful, sweet little person, so the next morning, I told my sisters and brother about what our [Pastor] had told me and that I was ashamed of myself and that I was going over to Town-ton's house. My sisters and brother followed me, and when Town-ton saw me, she ran out her house and leaped over their fence, her brothers and sister behind her, coming to meet [me] as if I was somebody. When Town-ton reached me with her family, all saying, 'We are so glad you came, Carria,' reaching out their [hands] to us, and we joyfully took their hands, saying, 'We love you,' over and over. Then Town-ton's family backed up and bowed to the ground before us, and we bowed. Her little family bowed in front of my little family. I didn't want to cry, but it was so beautiful, those little [people] bowing to each other. I tried hard not to cry, but I was so full of that wonderful sweet thing called love, I was hot like fire burning inside of me. I started crying out loud; for what it was about, I knew not, for I was just a little child and all of we little people were crying, and we had come together like a bunch of something. We were like a lot of plants growing together, thus forming themselves into a bunch. All you could hear was, 'I am sorry; I love you' 'I love you too.' By then, the people had begun to gather, for they thought we were fighting. My parents didn't know we had gone to Town-ton's house to say I am sorry and ask her to forgive me, but they were glad that we did. When those people who came to see, when they saw nothing but love, they left, saying, 'For sure, the Pastor had something to do with that.' Then Town-ton's father came over to us and bowed three times to me and [I] bowed three times to him too. He said, 'I am glad this thing happened, because I prayed to God to change your mind, because if a little vine is not checked right here where it first comes out of the ground, it will began to spread. You see one ant in your house today. The next day two or three if unchecked; in a month you will have to vacate that house, because ants will have taken it over.' I said, 'but Mister Wink King, it was only me, one person.' He replied, 'Yes, Little Pretty Love Bird, you are just one now, but that's all it takes to get started, Carria, just one. That's all, just one.' I bowed and said, 'I am so sorry, Mister Wink King.' He bowed, saying, 'That's what only love can do.'

Every little girl in town loved him then and never stopped loving him, can anybody tell me why? A little [girl] start beating on her Paw's leg, shouting, "Paw, I know! I know! I know!" Her Paw stood her on a table and said, "Tell us, baby." She yelled, "We girls loved him so much because he loved us so much. That's why Paw!" The people did want to keep applauding and yelling, "Praise the Lord!" over and over again saying, "That's what love can do." Then Town-ton began making signs with her eyes, so I looked back, and there was a tall, handsome, good-looking man coming toward us. Our heads bowed down, looking up grinning at each other, then we took off to him and she took one arm and I took the other and we walked over to where there [were] still a few folks, [he] saying, "My dear people, when you stop loving other people, you unconsciously began losing love for yourself, which causes one to die within, because hate is not only satanic, it is a spiritual crime against God."

The second day of the death of Pastor Johns had just begun, which is Friday -- the next day Saturday to be waked, and buried on Sunday. An old lady stood and said, "I found that this man was such a loving person that even if you didn't like him, you couldn't but respect the man. Some people had been heard saying it seems sometimes like he be asking Jesus for his cross in the kind of words he used in his prayer such as, 'Lord Jesus, let me carry a part of your cross, and even to suffer and die for your Church, if need be, Lord; if in your service for your people, [it] would be the greatest thing that could ever happen to me.' This old lady said, "Hey folks, you know what that man did?" With her face full of frowns one Sunday after noon Church service, she turned to another elderly lady who was the only sister of Pastor Johns, saying to Sister Johnane, "Would you please tell this [ ] you were right, dear?" She replied, "Yes Mam, Mo-mon, I'll be glad to." She said that was the saddest day of my life: "My older brother, God bless his soul, he did every thing but get on his knees begging us to try not to remember, spread, talk about, or even think about what they saw that day, not make a big thing or do any bragging, for if you love me, you will want to have me around a little longer, but if you spread this thing, the Almighty most high God will quickly move me out of his way, for God will have no person or thing get between him and his people." The paper reporter in charge came over to Sister Johnane -- his name was Mr. Maney. He said, "Sister Johnane, what in this world could this man have done so bad that he would want it concealed from the whole world? And not want to be remembered by? Or for?" Mister Maney went on to say, "Folks, we all know for a fact that if a man does some bad, he will want to hide it." Nobody opened their mouth. "But to the contrary, if he does some good, they want the world to hear about it, read it, and write about it." But the Pastor's sister got up, walked over to Mister Maney, and looked him in the eyes, moving her head from side to side saying, "Mister Maney, I am sorry; you just didn't know Pastor Johns, and you didn't know what kind of man God made him. But here is the story:

"One Sunday after our noon Church service, when we were letting out, there appeared two carloads of sheriffs and stopped in front of the Church, and in the twinkling of an eye, they were out of those cars with guns in their hands, which was a common occurrence for colored people. We don't like it, but that's the way it is down here. The sheriff that was in charge was a six-time killer, two in that year. He was known as "Big Joe;" [he] stood in front of the Church yelling, 'Get that young Nigger out here, or I am coming in there and shoot it out with him.' So Pastor Johns brought the young man outside, and stood in front of him, Mister Maney, and this sheriff was a commonly-known killer. Big Joe, he had over the years killed three Negro boys, three white boys, and one white woman. He raised his gun at him and pointing directly at him, 'I hate preachers, all of um, and that includes you, damn Nigger preacher,' saying, 'if you don't get from in front of that killer, I am going to shoot him down through you.' The Pastor said, 'Men of the Law, I am not going to move, and God don't want me to. But hear me out first, and when I finish, then you may start shooting, Mister Big Joe.' So he yelled to the rest of his murdering deputies to hold their fire. You see, Mister, they had come here to kill all of us the moment he (Big Joe) fired his gun. The Pastor went on, 'I heard about what went on among you hateful people last night about eight-thirty in town, and all of you know that at that time of night, no Negro or Non-white person would [be] found in that neighborhood where those three lawmen were shot dead. At six-o-clock, my wife and I left home on our way to the Church, stopping along the way, but Earl's mother asked us to wait for her and her son, Earl Lee,' -- who Big Joe wanted, along with us. 'We waited, and by the time we got to the Church, it was seven-fifteen. I know, because I looked at my watch when I opened the door, and we didn't leave until after nine-o-clock. The service was a little longer that night because it was so highly emotional. So you see, Sir, Mister Big Joe, Earl Lee could not have been in town killing sheriffs and be here in this Church at the same time.' The Pastor said, 'Now I am finished; you may start shooting, Mister Big Joe.' He replied, 'Now that you are finished telling that damn lie, I am going to count to ten and [if] you are still standing there, um goner kill you, and when you fall, um-mor laugh at you.' Smiling then, 'Um-mor take my time watching that little dirty Nigger-Sheriff-killer on his knees beg for his life before I kill him, and Preacher, that's the same as killing two mad dogs to me.' Then he began counting. When [he] said, 'eight,' Mister Maney, all of the people were turned looking at all of that dust up the road. Lo and Behold, there were coming carloads of deputy Sheriffs, and they ran up there and stopped, leaping out of their cars shouting, 'Big Joe, we got um!' Deputy Wiser came over to the Church, sat on the Porch, which was Big Joe's brother in-law. He married Big Joe's only sister, only living kin. Big Joe went over to him saying, 'Hey man, who were the killer?' Wiser, his sister's husband, bent his head. Then Big Joe, drawing his gun, saying, 'God-damnit, who are -- I have got to know!' Turning to him in deep sadness, tears running down his face, saying, 'Big Joe, it's my wife and my son, your only sister, and your only Nephew, and Ouercoa, your only best friend. They said they were going to get rid of you today, had they not been caught, and all three of them are charged [with] pre-meditated first-degree murder, and [my] job is gone and what am I going to do now, Joe? I ain't got no education, and I don't know how to do (nut-in) and Joe, now that everything that your sister have is tied up now -- all that boy ain't messed up -- now I ain't no more sheriff. They gave me one week to get lost or else, they told me already. I don't have nowhere to go and I ain't got no folks.' A week later, he was seen placing large rocks in his pockets alongside the river bank, when a colored man who was going fishing saw and went over to him, knowing what he was doing, to try to talk him out of killing himself, but he told the colored man, 'Can't you see I am a white man?' He replied, 'Yes Sir,' and went on fishing and watched that [man] fill his pockets and just walked down into the river and never came up. But Big Joe had gone and set on the side of the Church's porch with tears rolling down his face, and we all were crying out, but the members were crying out mostly in loving joy and thanksgiving that they still had their Pastor around. That white, colored, crazy, chosen man of God all in one body is still with us. The pastor was so full of compassion for Sheriff Wiser, his wife and son -- he used to say many times that compassion for a person, when real, is like giving bread to the hungry -- one of his deacons came over and sat beside him and said, 'Man, what are you crying about? Aren't you glad that that rat didn't kill you?' He looked at me and said, 'Brother deacon, don't you ever do that again; if [you] do, God won't like [it], and you will make him mad with you.' It wasn't what he said as [much as] it was the way he said it, so I said, 'Pastor, what did I do?' He replied, 'God did not make RAT. He made him a man just like you and me.' Then I said, 'Yes Sir, I am sorry; please pray for me."

and his [sister] Johnane looked over to the reporter, Mister Maney. So he rose and said, "Sister Johnane, you were right. I just didn't know Pastor Johns, and I wish I did. The men on the job just would not tell the kind of stories that I have been hearing here because they knew we were too damn hateful to believe anything good about a good man." A little Chinese girl said, "I was standing in front of my Pastor after he didn't get killed. I was so hurt and mad with that man who wanted to kill him, so [I] forced those words out by saying, 'Dear Pastor, do you still love those people and feel sorry for them?' He loved the little people so much he smiled and said, 'You see, Tin-tin, Baby Child, these people need help and I have what they need and can help them, but they are so obsessed with the word *White* until some of them actually think themselves to not just wearing the word *White* as a brand, but because they are actually, physically, or realistically white flesh, so you see, it is hard -- in some cases impossible. Some of them would rather lose their soul than to listen to a so-called non-white [who is?] saved. So now you see why I feel sorry for some of them, and I love all people. And you may ask what do those people could possibly need that they can't buy, such as Big Joe -- he has enough money to but anything.' I asked, 'What is there that big Joe can't buy?' He said, 'How many things do you want me to name?' 'Just one.' He said, 'How about Life? Christ? Love your own children? Health? Mind? I said, 'I see now, Pastor. Thank you."

Sister James, sitting on a blanket with her little family, stunned the people by coming to her feet, crying out aloud. Her husband and children tried to console [her], but she cried out saying, "I can remember as if it was yesterday. My little girl took sick, real sick, Mister Reporter, and it [was] just the time for the doctor to pass through here. He came to my house; he was in the village. When he checked, he asked a few things about for the last few days. Then he recognized her sickness, then said to me, 'I am sorry, James,' shaking his head from side to side, saying, 'This is a new disease; for a couple of years, it has been showing up all over the south. And medical science is trying to find some cure because it is killing so many children but has found nothing yet. I told him that she won't eat or drink anything, and her skin was as dry as a chip and the little thing was nothing but skin and bones. The doctor looked at me and said, 'I am sorry; there is nothing I can do. Almost four days with no food and water; the child is all but dead now. I give her not more then two days to live.' A little later that evening, I looked up and there was Pastor Johns picking up my little girl in his arms, and the people just looking and praying for him and walked out of the door and at his house, then went to the Church, where he stayed all night, and the next morning, I went to the door and saw a man and a woman walking in the road each holding a little girl's hand walking in between them, and I turned to go back into the house, and said, 'Hey----that's my little [girl!]'; and she screamed and fell out, and the people were yelling and shouting, "Praise the Lord!" "Thank God for that man, a servant of God and man, who served God by serving people!" [She] said he gave her the baby and said, "Feed her," and walked out where his wife was waiting for him, and "...here is that little sick girl eighteen [years] later, and nobody knows what he said to, as he put it the Almighty most high God, that he calls 'Father,' and now he is got all of us calling God 'Father,' and I am glad about [it], and at Sunday's service, the little gall was all over the Church. The Pastor looked at her, then looked up, saying, 'Lord Jesus, Thank You for doing this [for] me, and Lord if you want me to do anything for You, just let me know. You can find me right here under Your feet.' The next morning, I went to her bed to see how she was doing real early and she was already up and outside feeding the chickens."

An old lady who said she didn't know how old she was, but she knew it was more than a hundred for sure, she said, "Folks, I was there that day when my Pastor put that Bible verse into action that says, 'No greater love than this, that a [man] will lay down his life for his friend.' After that sheriff Big Joe could not, but really wanted to, kill [him], Pastor Johns was sitting on the Church porch, when sheriff Big Joe went over and sat beside him and put his arm around the pastor's shoulder and said, 'Preacher,' with tears running down his face, saying, 'I am glad now that you did what you did; you kept me from killing the poor young boy, but in the process, you almost got yourself killed. I really wanted to kill you because I hated all preachers and thought all of them were a bunch of frauds, but I couldn't pull that trigger, and now I am glad I couldn't.' The villagers were just standing around looking and listening when they heard Big Joe say, 'Preacher, we came here with blood in our eyes. The reason we wanted blood, and a lot of it, [was] because those three men who were law men just like us, men whom we worked with, and knew very well, are all dead now, killed in cold blood, and while we were making up our minds to start shooting y'all, just in time the other deputies were coming to tell us the killers were white people, and my only two living kin; my only sister, and my only nephew, but we thought it a Negro who did the killing, and we were coming here to just start paying for the blood of those three sheriffs, and it was not going to stop here, and God knows it wasn't going to stop for many years, to pay for all of that blood. We were going to start with your Pastor; we were going to kill him whenever or wherever we found him, and I don't know when we were going to stop the killing of your people.' A little girl about nine-years-old raised her hand, and he said, 'Yes?' She moved up a bit and said, 'Mister Sheriff Big Joe, why did y'all think it was a Negro who did such a terrible thing like that?' He replied, 'Baby,' smiling, 'because we have done you so much wrong that [we] just thought surely some of you killed to get even with us law men. 'But y'all ought to know that we don't do those kind of things; we haven't killed anybody since we been freed from owner-ship slavery, Sir.' Then raised his hands open, saying, 'Baby, you are right, because the man I killed from this village, I shot him in his mouth and stood over him asking him, 'Nigger, you still want to know why I stopped you?' He died praying, just moving his lips, and those people came to me telling me in as many words that they were [going] to lie for me, but did not see me murder a man in cold blood. I had never been [able] to understand until today how in this world that man could still love me while am murdering him for nothing but race-hate, in cold blood. You see, he was coming from -- I knew him, Bill Sanders; he used to come to our place on weekends and doctor on our animals. He was a nice person, and he knew a lot about animals. He was something like an animal doctor and he could do so many other things. He was younger then me, and I was about twenty-five years old then, and I didn't know how to do anything, so I guess out [of] malice, I stopped [him] on the road and was asking him all kind of stupid questions, trying to make him mad, but he was that kind of a person. He said, 'Mister Joe, you know me from a boy; why are you stopping me? Why the gun?' I didn't answer; I just killed that man because of the hate-disease I caught from my father, parents, and grand parents. Hate was their God; it's the only thing they worshiped and made their children do the same. When a child, the thing that bothered us was that we were not happy and had little child-like play time. Whenever we would pass through this and other such villages, it would make us sick of the stomach,' so Pastor said, 'Excuse me, please? Sir, would you please explain that statement? But I think we ought to all go inside the Church where we can all sit down,' so they did. Now that they were all comfortably seated inside, the Poor Millionaire Killer Sheriff Big Joe went on, '…and as I was saying about passing through here, we would seem to see happiness, joy, laughter, young women working in the gardens -- the children looked so healthy and full of play, running, jumping, play-fighting, and just playing all over the place, even racing like mad; men and women coming from Church holding hands, hugging each other with their show of happiness and joy, and we would say, 'Look at them damn Niggers with all of that love and religion and don't have anything else, not even real freedom or protection of the law in the whole country, and nor any money, land, or real education -- then why are they so damn happy? You tell me, Pastor." He replied, 'Sirs, the Bible says in the form of a question, 'What would it profit a person if they gain the whole world and [lose] their soul? It would profit them nothing, so if you I or anybody die right now, what we own …..' [end of manuscript]…….

Athur Mitchell

Arthur Mitchell was born in Irontown, Louisiana, on August 24, 1915. He moved to New Orleans at some time during his early childhood, where he grew up on St. Peter Street in the French Quarter. According to the manuscript, children "just did not run the streets at night in those days;" instead, he and his siblings sat around the coal or wood stove listening to their grandparents and other relatives, some of whom at that point were over a hundred years old and who had been born in slavery. Those stories without a doubt made a lasting impression on young Arthur, especially those concerning a man named Henry Goody Jons, born of a French immigrant farmer and a young slave girl he bought from the slave block in New Orleans in the year 1810. The eldest child of that union was Henry Goody Jons, who later changed his name to "Johns" after becoming pastor of Jons Town Baptist Church in Jons Town, La. According to Pastor Johns, he asked his paw for permission to change the spelling of his name because he was not then, "and never would be good enough" to carry the name of the church and town.

As Arthur Mitchell grew older, and became a pastor himself, the stories he heard in his childhood became more than just memories: to him, they became living legends and models of a way of life that he feared would eventually be lost to future generations. He felt compelled to preserve not only the stories themselves, but what those stories represented to his people and to their future. Mitchell's job at the Cabildo in New Orleans, where he began work in his early 20's, allowed him two 15-minute breaks each day, in addition to his lunch break. According to his daughter, Teryl, during his breaks, Mitchell would run up to the third floor, where he had a small table and chair, and he would write for 15 minutes at a time, putting on paper the stories he had heard from his relatives and grandparents. The resulting manuscript, occasionally edited by Mitchell himself when he was unsure of a spelling or the correct version of a name, is a remarkable document from a man who had only a fourth-grade education and who wrote in 15-minute segments.

What sets these stories apart from other chronicles of slavery is the story of a family captured along the shores of Lake Tanganyika, in East Central Africa. Few chronicles of African slavery in America actually begin with an account of the African way of life and with the capture itself; even fewer originate with a people who already knew how to read and write English and do basic mathematics. These slaves were advertised all over the South for their education in a time when few French farmers could boast of the same skills and when women running plantations on their own had need of slaves who could read and write. Even more importantly for the story, however, is the Christian education and principles of these slaves, principles that animated them even as they were being brought across the ocean in the hold of a slave-ship.

As a pastor himself, Arthur Mitchell appears to have modeled his ministry after that of Henry Good Jons. He worked for most of his life as a plumber and electrician, even while pastoring the Holy Bible Baptist Church, a church he built with his own hands on Delery Street in the lower ninth ward of New Orleans. After Hurricane Betsy (in 1965), Mitchell helped repair the homes in St. Bernard Parish, where he was living. Later, he went to work at the Cabildo as a plumber, retiring in 1989. He continued to serve as Pastor of his church until he was 79 years old, five years before he died in August 2000. According to his widow, Ms. Josephine, "Mitchell" got the young people to help him in the church, and he "captured their hearts" because he spent time with them and did things with them no one else wanted to do. He often cooked in the church -- beans and rice, hamburgers, etc. -- and would serve meals to the young people after the Tuesday and Thursday night Bible Studies. He had a camper that he used to take the kids out camping, and he would often visit the Senior Citizen Nursing Home on St. Maurice St., or invite those who could come to his house for fried chicken, cake, and drinks on Sunday afternoons.

Mr. Mitchell built not only his own church, but his own house as well, a house that still stands among the utter destruction in the area wrought by Hurricane Katrina. Although the house was inundated by flood waters from the levee break just a few blocks away, it did not shift on its foundation as did most of the houses in that area, a testimony, according to Ms. Mitchell, to the work of her husband. The house has been mostly repaired, and is the place where Mrs. Mitchell still resides and cares for herself at 86 years of age.